RESEARCH IN INDOLOGY
A NEW PERSPECTIVE

Edited
by
Dr. Rabindra Kumar Panda

BKP

BHARATIYA KALA PRAKASHAN
DELHI (INDIA)

Published by:
C.P. Gautam
Bharatiya Kala Prakashan
3611/5, Narang Colony,
Tri Nagar, Delhi-110035
Ph. 7192770

First Published : 1998

Ed. Dr. Rabindra Kumar Panda

ISBN :- 81-86050-22-1
Price : Rs. 500.00

Laser Typesetting by
Ishan Comprint
G 16/14, Qutab Enclave-I, (DLF)
Gurgaon (H.R.), Ph. 8-352412

Printed at
Santosh Offset Press
40, Anand Nagar, Inder Lok, Delhi-110035

DEDICATED
To The Sweet Memory of
My Grand Father & Grand Mother
Late Yogi Panda
&
Late Kamala Panda

Advance in knowledge is essentially distinction, not aggregation. Each new particular of knowledge is not an addition, but a newly observed part of a previously conceived whole.

JOHN GROTE
Exploratio Philosophical
II, 299.

CONTENTS

PREFACE

Research implies, in essence, the critical and scientific inquiry and the seeking of all possible evidence that might throw light on the real meaning of a text, a fact, a concept, a school of thought etc.

Research is a scientific undertaking which, by means of logical and scientific methods, aims to discover new facts or verify old facts, and to analyse their sequence, interrelationships and the factors which govern them. Research is, therefore, a careful and critical study or examination in seeking facts or principles. It is an intelligent and diligent investigation in order to ascertain something. It answers questions by the accumulation and assimilation of generalisations, corrects or verifies knowledge. Research is an intellectual act that starts with the asking of a question and progresses through the critical and analytical study of evidence and arrives at new conclusions or new knowledge. As per Webster's *New International Dictionary* (2nd ed., London, Eell and Sons, 1959) (Research may have the following objectives which are as follows):

(a) To find new generalisation with old data;

(b) To know old conclusions with new data;

(c) To attempt to reach more conclusions from the same set of data;

(d) To put forward an entirely original idea, or to discover an unexplored horizon of knowledge.

(e) To find or to resolve contradictions existing in the area of study; and

(f) To continuously develop a discipline or field of study, with the use of scientific and rational methods.

Hence research is necessary to examine the extent of the validity of the old conclusions or to find out some new facts and generalisations in connection with the existing ones. It purports to give a new direction and a new insight into the existing problem and therefore a means to the advancement of knowledge in any discipline of knowledge.

Though Indian Universities have made valuable contributions to

Indological Research, we are still lagging behind as far as Sanskrit research is concerned. The reasons for this are not too far to be identified, the main being:

Traditional methods of teaching, and lack of research orientation;

Absence of knowledge about research methodology;

Inadequate strength of the departments and Institutions in Sanskrit Viswavidyalayas, Vidyapeethas, which are overburdened with doing classroom teaching;

Non-availability of many qualified research supervisors;

Selection of inefficient, indifferent, and disinterested persons;

Inadequate financial support;

Lack of good library facilities and availability of necessary informative materials;

Absence of essential data;

Entry of majority students to research, from an academic background which does not prepare them for this specialised activity;

Lack of incentives for doctorates;

Absence of identification of research areas.

The increasing interest and aptitude for research deserve encouragement, direction, financial assistance, and co-ordination. It requires a concentrated endeavour on the part of the institutions which are related directly or indirectly with teaching and research. A few suggestions are given below to accelerate the speed of important and qualitative research in our country.

1. On the patterns of the CSIR, ICAR, ICMR, ICSSR, ICPR, a national body, ICSR (Indian Council of Sanskrit Research) should be set up. This can identify research areas; formulate national research policies, design and co-ordinate research activities; and work as a clearing house. It should be established with responsibilities for monitoring, indexing and abstracting research reports, conferences and Seminar proceedings, Journals and other publications in the field.
2. Association of Sanskrit Research centres should be set up. This can be entrusted with the work of disseminating the results of Sanskrit research through a newsletter.

Indological Research Round Table (IRRT) should be established. Its main objectives could be (a) to contribute towards the extension and improvement of Indological research; (b) to provide oppertunities for discussing, disseminating and evaluating Indological research projects; and (c) to orient and educate Indological personel and professonals concerning relevant research, research methods and their usefulness. The IRRT could have an Information Exchange Cell which can provide a platform for presenting and discussing the completed, in-progress, and proposed research. Any individual, Institution, research centre organisation interested in Indological research could become a member of the IRRT.

There must be provision for information packages (standard researches) on topics of relevance relating to Indological education, with detailed research project descriptions.

An annual list of completed research at the Ph.D., M. Phil., D.lit. levels should be issued. Similarly, a register of current research in Indology in India and abroad should also be established. This work may be alloted to one or two Indological teaching departments or Oriental Research Institutes.

Research in Indology in India should be made the theme of an All India Seminar or All India Oriental Conference. In this, bibliographical organisation of research, dissemination of research, national research policy, funding of research, publication of research reports etc., could be discussed thoroughly and a consensus could be arrived at. All efforts and persuasion must be made to see that the recommendations of such a seminar are implemented in the real sense of the term.

There is much improvement needed in respect of the subjects taken up for research. There is a tendency to select easy subjects or to go over familiar ground again. Among the many Śāstras, Vedānta and Purāṇa are most frequently chosen. There is less attention paid to the earlier and more important phases of the growth of the different Śāstras, about which material is meagre, and not readily available. Vedic Research is on the whole very much neglected. On Vedic Ritual and the Kalpa-Sūtras there is very little work done. Indo-European Linguistics is a neglected area of Research. The ample materials of the Purāṇas are still to be exploited in full. A lot of confusion still exists in respect of the varied contents of most of the Purāṇa-texts, which all need to be completely edited afresh in a critical manner, after a full survey of their manuscripts and recensions. With Purāṇas goes the equally large corpus of texts of Āgama, Tantra and similar Saṁhitā Literature, Navya-Nyāya and certain aspects of Vyākaraṇa offer subjects of semantic and symbolic logic, are special areas to which attention needs to be directed.

Various problems relating to Buddhism and Jainism need to be tackled afresh in the light of the new material that is being brought to light. Indian Sociology has to be properly studied so that today, when the nation is passing through great changes, there may be a better understanding of the ideology underlying the traditional patterns. Folk Culture, as reflected in Sanskrit literature, is another attractive subject. In Alaṁkāra, General Aesthetics requires further investigation. In literature proper, a Dictionary of Sanskrit literature is a desideratum. Forms and phases of Sanskrit as a medium of expression, such as Vedic Epic, Narrative, Epigraphical, Buddhistic, Jaina, literary, Philosophical, technical and so on need to be examined from the points of view of grammar, diction, vocabulary etc. Similarly, the study of Sanskrit in relation to the Modern Indo-Aryan and the Dravidian and Pre-Dravidian languages forms yet another line demanding further attention.

In the domain of Art, work in Nāṭya, Sangita and Śilpa, including Architecture, Iconography and Painting, has been almost negligible. All the scientific subjects - Āyurveda, Jyotiṣa, Gaṇita - deserve to be taken up. Among themes of wider interest are Sanskrit Epigraphy, Ancient Indian Geography, Nīti and Arthaśāstra, Indian games and pastimes, Ancient Festivals and the like.

Another new line of work which we may usefully adopt from America is the interdisciplinary study, where a specific general subject is studied and discussed by scholars belonging to different disciplines from different points of view, such as language, Religion, Sociology, Economics and so on. This is of great help in developing a whole view of a subject. In Indology, there are several subjects which can be tackled like this from the points of view of different Śāstras. In connection with more general questions also, such as those pertaining to Indian culture, institutions, phases of thought etc., such an Interdisciplinary approach is bound to derive much light from the ideals and ideologies embodied in Sanskrit and Prakrit works.

The present volume is the first fruit of my on going major project 'RESEARCH IN INDOLOGY' sanctioned by SARASVATI, Sanskrit Akademi of Research for Advanced Society through Vedic and allied Tradition of India, Bhuvanesvara. The objective of the project is to make an appraisal of Indological research of various kinds taking into consideration the growth of Indological research in its size, significance, relevance and scope over the years in response to the needs of professionalism and the socio-economic developmental demands. On the basis of the findings of such a type of investigation it is proposed to bring to light the needs, problems and other issues related with the process of present day Indological research. It is hoped that such an investigation will help us in realising the problems and to solve them. It will give us new direction and guideline in changing the present trend and improving the quality of research in the field of Indology.

The present volume is a partial result of the investigation. It contains the reflections, suggestions and views on some aspects of contemporary research in Indology. In this volume twenty critical research papers are included. The volume is divided into two sections. The first section embodies the papers which are based on research needs and problems. The scholars have attempted to show the problems and have suggested the ways to solve them. Prof. M. Srimannarayana Murti in his paper, Principle of Recurrence in Indian Mythology suggests that the aim of Indological research is to know the past as much precisely as possible of our Indian nation with a view to recapture the mentality and atmosphere and to connect what is good in the past with the present. He emphasises on the principle of recurrence for getting in-depth knowledge of the Mythological works. Prof. Dash has suggested the future fields of Sanskrit research and training such as Computer and Sanskrit studies, women studies in Sanskrit, Pilgrimology and Tourism, Culturology and Rituology and Futurology. Dr. Rajendran has given some very important suggestions for revamping Indological Research. Dr. Ghosh has shown the usefulness of ancient methodology in Indian philosophical research. Dr. Moghe has made a critical survey of three decades of the studies of Dharmaśāstra and presented the results of his study. Dr. Misra has shown the relevance and direction of Vedic study in Modern India. Dr. Swain has suggested that there is enough source material for Indological research in Sanskrit. How a standard work of Indology can claim the status of scientific research is shown by him in a methodological manner. Dr. Mahapatra analyses the needs and problems of Indological research. Dr. Vartak has given us new light in his paper by showing how astronomy can be of help to fix the dates of Sanskrit texts such as *Rāmāyana* and *Mahābhārata*. Dr. N.K. Dash has made a comparison between Tibetology and Indological Studies. Dr. Sweta Prajapati has shown us some neglected areas of Sanskrit research. Miss Preeti Adhiya has discussed how Alaṁkāraśāstra is an important area of research in Sanskrit.

The second section contains some articles based on textual studies. The scholars have given us valuable fruits of their independent investigation in form of papers included in this volume.

The work realises us that there should be serious study on the research; the problems standing on the way of its development should be brought to light; needs of Indological research should be realised in proper perspective and above all qualitative and relavant research should be made.

However, Indology as a discipline has been steadily growing in its size, significance and scope over the years in response to the needs of professonalism and the diverse socio-economic developmental demands. With the growth of this discipline, the research of various kinds in this important branch of knowledge has been significantly increased and is at present in the speed of rapid growth. This has opened scope for an important area of research i.e. critical appraisal of the researches keeping in view problems and issues involved with the process of research. This will bring to light some interesting facts which will be definitely helpful to us to think in new direction and in bringing out changes in our research perspective. I have therefore, undertaken a project to investigate and to explore this area. As a part of this undertaking, a volume of articles/ research papers; entitled *Research in Indology* is now seeing the light of the day. The objective of the volume is to present views/suggestions/critical observations/ comments/ reflections of the prominent scholars on important aspects of indological Research. I hope the present volume will give new direction and guidance to the young and talented researchers and will be received by the scholarly world.

While presenting this volume to the readers I naturally remember with gratitude the co-operation and support extended by several persons, in the absence of which this volume would not have seen the light of the day. A word of thanks is too meagre, while not uttering even that is grossly improper. However, a word of special thanks is due to

— the authors of the papers for their contribution to the present volume.

— the scholars who had inspired and motivated to undertake this work

— my wife Sweta and my sister Sasmita for editorial work, typing and proof-reading.

— the publisher, C.P Gautam, Bharatiya Kala Prakashan, Delhi and his staff for efficiently bringing out the publication in the present form.

R.K. Panda

CONTRIBUTORS

1. M. Srimannarayana Murti
   Professor & Director
   Oriental Research Institute
   Sri Venkateswara University
   Tirupati-517 502
   Andhra Pradesh
2. Keshab Chandra Dash
   Head Deptt. of Nyaya Philosophy
   Sri Jagannatha Sanskrit Vishvavidyalaya
   Shrivihar, Puri-752 002
   Orissa
3. C. Rajendran
   Professor & Head
   Deptt. of Sanskrit,
   University of Calicut
   Kerala
4. Raghunatha Ghosh
   Deptt. of Philosophy
   University of North Bengal
   Dt. Darjeeling-734 430
   West Bengal
5. S. G. Moghe
   Retd. Professor of Sanskrit
   74-B Tatya Gharpure Path
   J.S.S. Road,
   Mumbai-400 004
6. Vasant Parikh
   Retd. Professor of Sanskrit
   Opp. Lohana Building, Amareli
   Gujarat

7. Madhusudana Mishra
P.G. Deptt. of Sanskrit
G.M. College
Sambalpur
Orissa-768 004

8. B.K. Swain
Reader & Head
Dept. of Dharmasastra
Sri Jagannatha Sanskrit Visvavidyalaya
Sri Vihar, Puri-752002
Orissa

9. Gopinatha Mohapatra
Professor of Sanskrit
Nila Sadma
Santarapur Road
Bhubaneswar-751 002,
Orissa

10. Vartak Padmakar Vishnu
Medical Doctor
521, Shaniwar Peth
Pune-411030
Maharastra

11. Sweta Prajapati
Research Officer
Oriental Institute
M.S. University of Baroda
Baroda-390 002

12. Rabindra Kumar Panda
Lecturer
Dept. of Sanskrit, Pali & Prakrit
Faculty of Arts,
M.S. University of Baroda
Baroda - 390 002
Gujarat

13. Narendra Kumar Dash
Lecturer
Dept. of Indo-Tibetan Studies
Vishvabharati University
Calcutta, West Bengal

14. Preeti Adhiya
Research Scholar
Dept. of Sanskrit, Pali & Prakrit
Faculty of Arts
M.S. University
Baroda-390 002

15. Bijayananda Kar
Professor & Head
Dept. of Philosophy
Utkal University, Vani Vihar
Bhubaneswar
Orissa

16. Achyautananda Dash
Lecturer,
Dr. Harishing Gaur Visvavidyalaya
Sagar
Madhya Pradesh

17. S.G. Moghe
Retd. Professor of Sanskrit
74-B, Tatya Ghar Pure Path
J.S.S. Road
Mumbai-400 004

18. Nirmala Kulkarni
Research Scholar
Centre of Advanced Study in Sanskrit
University of Poona
Pune, Maharashtra

19. K.H. Hota
Lecturer,
Sanskrit Dictionary Department
Deccan College

Yerawada
Pune-411006
Maharashtra

20. A. Ramanna
Lecturer in Sanskrit,
Osmania University,
Hyderabad-500 007

SECTION

I

1

PRINCIPLE OF RECURRENCE IN INDIAN MYTHOLOGY

M. Srimannarayana Murti

Our aim of research in Sanskrit is to know the past as much precisely as possible of our Indian nation with a view to recapture the mentality and atmosphere and to connect what is good in the past with the present. For a correct comprehension of the Vedic, perhaps of the Indo-Aryan and even of the Indo- European cultures, there is a need to read together the *Vedas, Rāmāyaṇa, Mahābhārata,* Purāṇas, Kalpa and legal literatures. None of these texts are adequate in themselves. For example, the Saṁhitā, Bhāhmaṇa, Āraṇyaka and Upaniṣadic portions of the Vedic literature are not of the same date and indeed they represent different epochs in the ancient Indian cultural evolution. Various recensions of the four Vedas are also lost irrecoverably and hence the extant texts are not even homologous. Further, these texts do not provide enough illustrations, save a few anecdotes eulogizing some thing on hand. The epics and *purāṇas* are mythologies, wherein too much of imagery is suspected to play. Even in spite of the extensive loss to the records and the available records are of unconfirmed nature, they cannot be rejected outright at least upto the period in which the epigraphs and archaeological survivals are available. Thus the historicity of these records should be established by adopting a balanced and scientific methodology.

The culture is always in change; but this change in an evolutionary society is sequential and hence all the facts are to be arranged scientifically. For example, what is said crisply in the *Veda* is elaborated with anecdotes, legends and long narratives in the epics and mythologies. The *Vālmīki- Rāmāyaṇa* stands midway between the sacrifical literature, (comprising the prayers (*saṁhitās*), the doctrine of sacrifice (*brāhmaṇas*) and the auxiliaries (*vedāṅgas*) and the philosophical literature (*āraṇyakas* and *upaniṣads*). These elaborations of the *Vālmīki-Rāmāyaṇa* are again abstracted into the rules in the Kalpa-sūtras and Dharmaśāstras. Again the same things are revised with new illustrations in the *Mahābhārata* and *Purāṇas*. Further, all the changes which occurred in the period of each composition are incorporated. Thus all these texts when read together show the evolution of the Indian cultural history which is characterised by continuous search for finding a balance in the material, mental and spiritual aspects of life against the ideas and ideals, about the conduct of human beings and the social institutions with a formidable belief in transmigration and destiny.

Mythology is the main source to know the expansion of culture. As the word *myth* suggests, mythology contains an elaborated account including imagery built upon some truth. The fabrication around truth couched in poetry is to lead the man to the path of life as conceived to be ideal in given times. In the *Veda* are two types of sentences called *vidhi* 'injunction' and *arthavāda* 'eulogy'. *Vidhi* is a fact and *arthavāda* is a myth. In the *Purāṇas* the tone of injunction is softened and subsumed with eulogy. Thus the roots of mythology were already formed in the Vedic literature itself as evident from the diverse versions of the Vṛttra-legend in different texts. So also the genesis of the Purāṇic narrations is found in the Veda itself. For example, Viṣṇu is praised in the *Ṛgveda* (1.154. 2-3) as a mighty god with a huge body - in which the universe rests and the living beings rejoice, and as having measured out the universe just by three strides. Viṣṇu is a subordinate divinity to Indra in the *Ṛgveda* and later in the Purāṇic period he becomes an independent divinity with all the characteristic features of Indra. So when Rāma is elevated as an incarnation of Viṣṇu, the *Brahmavaivartapurāṇa* (4.2 116. 20-22) identifies Rāma with Viṣṇu, Indra and also the five Pāṇḍava brothers, and Sītā with Draupadī. Similarly three strides of Viṣṇu in the *Ṛgveda* developed into Viṣṇu's incarnation as Trivikrama-Vāmana in the *Bhāgavata* (8.19).

As mentioned already, around the kernel of the story many changes are made in mythology by transporting the theme to the current situations with modifications and imageries. 'Theme' is basic cultural concept behind the abstractions and narrations. In the *Ṛgveda* (10.103.1-2) the brave wife Indrasenā drives the chariot of her husband Mudgala when his cattle were stolen by the robbers. In the *Bhāgavata* (10.59) Satyabhāmā drives the chariot of Kṛṣṇa when he waged a war against

Narakāsura. Some times the narration may be repeated with different personages in order to focus different aspects of human life. For example, the *Aitareya-bhāhmaṇa* (33.4) gives the episode of Śunaḥśepa with Ajīgarta Sauyavasi as his father, Viśvāmitra as the priest and Hariścandra Vaidhasa as the sacrificer. In the *Vālmīki- Rāmāyaṇa* (1.60 & 61) the story of Śunaḥśepa is narrated with the Ayodhyā king Ambarīṣa, Viśvāmitra and Ṛcīka as sacrificer, priest and father respectively. While the aim of the Śunaḥśepa episode in the *Aitareya-brāhmaṇa* is to repudiate the moral sense of the priest Ajīgarta, it is in the *Vālmīki-Rāmāyaṇa* to eulogize the virtues of Viśvāmitra.

Another salient feature of Indian literature is that it is never viewed as an art for art sake. The poeticians and doctrinists of all philosophical schools condemn alike literature which is not based on *dharma* 'religious order', let what religion it may be, and come forward with tabus like *kāvyālāpaṁśca varjayet* 'reading of literature is to be avoided'. Thus every literary composition reflects certain religious implications and contemporary beliefs, customs, etc. But because of the play of imagery, the cultural materials are to be gleaned with great care and restraint, keeping away all personal prejudices. When studies are carried out in restricted limits with defined methods of interpretation, the historicity of the epics and *Purāṇas* can also be established with certainty. All the imageries are to be judiciously omitted and conclusions are to be drawn on the basis of the kernel of the legend. Hence the guiding principle to identify the kernel is recurrence of themes.

Recurrence of theme is a safe principle for analysing the mythology as it is prefigured by the change in culture. Change in culture is warranted by socio-economic conditions like the division of labour, political overtones, foreign influences, food habits, etc. For example, division of labour leads to the division of society into classes on the basis of economic status and professional specialization. It results in strife and strife in its turn begets change in different social institutions. So some of the social practices become obsolete, some migrate to other places and some new ones are evolved by the people. New practices start as trends and stabilize as norms with the acceptance of the majority in the community. In fact several trends die in the middle for want of popular acceptance. The literature, mythology in particular, is the only source for obtaining the transitory trends and changing norms. Further the change, as a rule, of customs, beliefs, superstitions, morals and ethics proceed in a particular pattern. This is confirmed by the recurrence of themes in the literary compositions belonging to a given period or occurring in a time sequence. Hence *'recurrence of theme'* is a sound criterion to adjudge whether a given social practice is a trend or a norm. The normatic practices are described time and again in a book, by way of repetition with same or different persons. Similarly they are found repeated in the books of the respective contemporary times or of same genre.

The social norms are abstracted in the ritual and legal literatures and elaborated with illustrations in the forms of legends in mythology. The heroes, heroines and situations may be different, but the norms of the society remain to continue till they are antiquated by more recent ones. Such periodic appearance of the theme is called *"principle of recurrence"*. On other words the principle of recurrence is a phenomenon of the movement of themes in literature. This helps extremely in analysing the mythic data on the basis of the recurrence of the norms of society in a given poem or in a batch of poems of common genre. Myth is "a fable or legend embodying the convictions of people as to their gods or other divine personages, their own origin and early history and the heroes connected with it, or the origin of the world" (Webster). For example, all the *Purāṇas* aim at giving geneologies of various dynasties. But each *Purāṇa* omits some names of kings in each dynasty and focus with legendary account of some kings whose actions have either agitated or assured calmness in the society, with a view to emphasise the need for change in human behaviour. Even though each *Purāṇa* is inadequate in itself, all of them put together afford necessary historicity to the events in the cultural history. Therefore all the geneologies are to be combined and read together. For instance, the name Janaka for Sītā's father is patronymic while Sīradhvaja is his personal name. This becomes clear only by combining the geneologies given in the *Rāmāyaṇa* (1.70 3ff) and the *Viṣṇupurāṇa* (4.5). Similarly Janaka's brother is called Kuśadhvaja. The derivative conventional sense of the names Sīradhvaja and Kuśadhvaja also refer to the agricultural revolution brought by them in their kingdom, thus making the episodes of Sītā and Ahalyā as much meaningful as of Vṛttra in the Vedic period.

Let us take for illustration the theme of abduction of a married woman in the institution of marriage in the epics and *Purāṇas*. This will account for historically how the status of women was changing from time to time, until Manu came forward with several statutory measures and sanctions to protect women from exploitation.

Freedom enjoyed by women in the Vedic period came to be gradually restricted in several ways. The *Mahābhārata*, *Viṣṇupurāṇa* and *Bhāgavata* give legal clearance for abducting an unmarried girl with an intention to marry, as known from the marriage episodes of Vicitravīrya and Rukmiṇī. The *Vālmīki- Rāmāyaṇa* evidences for the existence of different rules regarding the abduction of a married woman. In Ayodhyā kingdom a man can discard his wife when they cannot live under one roof for any reason, in which case the woman gets freedom to remarry any person of her choice or live independently. So Rāma could leave his wife Sītā in the forest abducting his kingdom on learning adverse public opinion regarding the character of Sītā and his disposition towards her. The *Mārkaṇḍeya-purāṇa* (69) narrates that the king Uttama has discarded his wife Bahulā in the forest for being displeased with her behaviour whereas a married woman cannot be abducted for marriage or seduction in Ayodhyā. Abduction of and adultery with a married woman is a cognizable offence. Violation attracts punishment without warranty. The husband and the state being represented by the king and his personnel bear responsibility to provide protection to women under seduction. So Rāma felt an obligation to release not only Sītā but also Rumā, the wife of Sugrīva from their abductors Rāvaṇa and Vālin respectively. Whereas in Daṇḍaka forest and Laṅkā, a wife of another person can be abducted as much as an unmarried woman to marry or subdue her at consent. So in the *Rāmāyaṇa* Sītā is abducted by a demon Virādha soon after entering into the forest and Rāvaṇa in Pañcavaṭī. Similarly Vālin did not suspect any reason for Rāma to harm him when Sugrīva went to Kiṣkindhā-pura along with the latter and called him for a dual (4. 13ff). In order to enforce the law of Ayodhyā, Rāma proclaims Janasthāna, Kiṣkindhā and Laṅkā as falling in the territories of Ayodhyā kingdom (4.18.6 & i; 7.42.14). In the same way in the *Mārkaṇḍeya-purāṇa* (79 & 70) one brahmin by name Suśarman Vaiśālī approaches the king Uttama to help him to restore his wife who was abducted by one Rākṣasa by name Valāka in dead night. Valāka prevented her in Utpalāvartaka forest. Like Sugrīva, Uttaına helps

Suśarman to release her from the demon Valāka. Valāka is a good demon like Bali. The son Virocana and he abducted her to prevent Suśarman from performing his religious rituals. So he returned her to the king in obedience to the laws of the land for himself being domiciling in his territory (70.13). After Suśarman's wife is restored, Uttama also desired to get back his wife Bahulā. Uttama's wife was picked up in the forest by one Nāga king Kapotaka and took her to Pātāla with a view to marry her like Rāvaṇa. But Kapotaka's daughter Nandā hides her from him to avoid her to turn a rival cowife to her mother (71.20). Valāka helps to rescue her from Pātāla. These episodes are based on one common theme, namely position of a married woman in abduction, in the light of which Manu's wisdom in his laws on women can be appreciated.

In this way all the mythological data can be assembled and analysed by applyng the principle of recurrence. The assemblage of facts on a given theme describes a state of affairs but not truth. Now the phenomenological, philosophical and historical methods of research are to be employed, either each one separately or collectively, to ascertain truth. For obtaining best results both the approbative and ecensurable actions of the past are to be taken alike dispassionately. Lessons are to be taken to emulate zealously what was good yesterday and to shun what was bad meticulously.

As our country is basically evolved on formidable faith in rebirth and liberation, any thing, good or bad, can be communicated even to the man of common parlance by taking him to our cultural heritage. For example, Raja Ram Mohun Roy could bring into effect the abolition of Satī in Bengal by reinterpreting all the passages quoted by the *prima facie* and refuting all the sanctions. The Sanskrit studies become meaningful only when antisocial practices are stopped to recur again today and harmony is ensured in spite of superficial differences emanated from new modes of life brought by the advancement of science and technology.

2

FUNCTIONAL SANSKRIT : THE FUTURE FIELD OF SANSKRIT RESEARCH AND TRAINING

Keshab Chandra Dash

The fact remains that Leibniz, Mādhava, Newton, Nīlakaṇṭha and others made the same descoveries, the Indians even earlier. And yet, India did not only fail to experience a scientific revolution; it did not even produce a scientific mini- revolution".

F. Stall (1995):
"The Sanskrit of Science."

India has her own vision of science and her own conception of rationality. Indian notion of theoretical rationality, since it takes its basis from causal factors, it is not different from the scientific rationality of the West.

Ancient Indian science constitutes a far more practical and sensible way of meeting the essential needs of our people. There exists a rich corpus of theories, concepts and ideas in our ancient treatises which, if properly understood, re-interpreted, re-evaluated and utilised in the contemporary context can make substantial contribution to most of our productive endeavours. Further, with this indigenous traditional resource base a fresh beginning can be made with an aim of developing functional significance of our own sciences traditionally handed down to us through Sanskrit from time immemorial.

At the present state of affairs when people hear about Sanskrit they take the matter very losely and think that Sanskrit is just an ancient picture having no practical bearing on present living and life style. But some questions occur in the mind of a conscious few, such as : What does Sanskrit relate to? Why is this name *Sanskrit*? Who has connected this name with a language ? What are the reasons? Whether it is *Samskritā bhāṣā* (superfined language) or *Samskriti bhāṣā* (language of culture) ? Or is it used for both ? Who were the native speakers ? There may be some other questions like this.

It is needless to say that Sanskrit serves as a life force in India even today. It verily aims at achieving a national character and an integral fabric of Indian mind. What we need at present, is to restructure, rebuild and creatively vitalize Sanskrit for practical purposes and bring those elements afront that are conducive to scientific insights and ensure a balanced as well as a progressive living.

Sanskrit education as conceived by academic planners has been planned only to produce language teachers. Now it has lost its goal. There is also a shift in emphasis. With advancement of modern technologies there is a growing demand for rediscovering the technical aspect of Sanskrit. It is worth-noting that there was a time when Om (*Aum*) found its first revelation as an element of sound technology and most of the Śāstras (sciences) came into existence to fulfil the need of our society. In view of this, the objectives and perspectives of Sanskrit education need a redoing.

Recently there is an emphasis on vocational courses in the education pattern. We must appreciate the need and accordingly design some courses of Sanskrit from school level to post- graduate level along with some Diploma courses. We have to identify certain areas of functional Sanskrit and relate those to the fresh line of modern purpose. The following areas may be considered important for a beginning.

Communicative Sanskrit

Computer and Sanskrit Studies

Sanskrit Teaching Methodology

Ancient Indian Sciences and Technologies

Women Studies in Sanskrit

Yoga and Health Care

Spiritual Science

Pilgrimology and Tourism

Culturology and Rituology

Futurology

Communicative Sanskrit

Many people think that Sanskrit was never spoken and cannot be spoken also. Some others hold that why should be a communicative Sanskrit when there are mother tongues and other languages for inter-state communication. This is true, but now we are in search of a national character and a clear Indian identity. This can be achieved through communicative Sanskrit easily because this involves 60 to 70 words of mother tongue and some simple grammatical structures very close to that of mother tongues in India. Researches to this effect have been conducted and proved successful. The only thing remains that the courses so designed and developed need overall implementation.

Computer and Sanskrit Studies

Computational Sanskrit emerges as a new area of research and training. The techniques and methodologies developed in Sanskrit have been proved useful for both data-based and rule based operations in computer. The area is so sensitive that it would ensure a quick adaptability if development projects are planned to adjust the modern requirements like inter-lingua translation schemes and such other programmes in its basis.

Methodology of Sanskrit Teaching

Teaching of Sanskrit from school level to University level seems very much defective as it has no aim at all. Sanskrit is a vast field which covers various branches of learning. There are many subjects which lead to different types of theories, concepts and crises that build the structure of respective systems. The method of teaching Sanskrit as a language cannot be the same as that of a subject. Since Sanskrit has been reduced to be a classical language only by the planners there is a great confusion in designing the courses of studies. Sanskrit, therefore, fails to accomodate itself either as a language or as a subject. A scientific methodology for teaching different aspects of Sanskrit needs to be developed.

Ancient Indian Sciences and Technologies

F. Staal (1995) observes : "The world, therefore, does not know that India experienced not only a creative, an *Achsenzeit* or 'axial age' as has been the fashionable term, in the wider philosophical, cultural and religious sense at the time of Buddha and the *Upaniṣads*, but also, at about the same time a scientific revolution in which Pāṇini occupied the place of honour. It may be unfortunate that the world does not know that but it is fortunate that Sanskritists have made information about Indian grammar available and so contributed to the origin of Western Linguistics."

"In mathematics, we have a puzzle. India did not lack mathematical genius. Indian mathematics has not only a brilliant history with contributions ranging from Zero to algebra, it also produced discoveries on a par with those of Newton, the paragon of Western science and other pacemakers of Europe's Scientific revolution, people whose names are constantly on everyone's lips, unlike the names of Mādhava or Nīlakaṇṭha."

Incidentally, Staal remarks : "Why did the scientific revolution take place in Europe and not in India?"

With reference to above I want to stress the fact that there should be some courses of indigenous Indian science and modern scientists should be involved to take up some venture and some projects to rediscover the key for making an indigenous scientific revolution.

Women Studies in Sanskrit

As far as the Indian society is concerned the peace and progress of a family mostly depend upon a woman who is supposed to play a vital role in moulding and building its shape through her education, vision and uniform execution of discipline. Sanskrit possesses an intense amount of indegenous study materials especially for women to improve the quality of life and the skills that we actually need. To this effect some sorts of programmes should be chalked out.

Yoga and Health Care

In recent human enquiries, Yoga has emerged as a science to unfold the mysteries and various dimensions of mind. It also ensures a systematic growth of body. When there is a constant demand for a balanced and better living why do we fail to give a practical tool like Yoga to the society in general ? We have adequate experimental theories in Sanskrit that may be brought to limelight for broader comprehension, analysis and application.

Spiritual Science

Indian society is moving towards a total collapse in terms of morality. Corruption has become a demonic way of life from which nobody has an escape. People are actually in search of a new model of life or a fresh world-view in which life is supposed to be held high in point of potentiality of mind or intellect and actions. This is only possible if spiritual dimension of a man remains open and firm. Spiritual humanity is a lasting contribution of India to the world. If this remains in fact in practice many new wings of vision would flower to yeild productions and nothing would be there to sermonize in the name of morality. The Vedic studies and Darshanas should be directed for a persistent urging for spiritual humanity and its practical base in their scheme of course-making and research.

Pilgrimology and Tourism

Spiritual Centres have some positive roles to play in Indian life. Pilgrimage from one centre to another has been enhancing the environment of integration in India. But the mission is lost in chaos due to lack of essential awareness, channels of information, communication skills of those who lead and guide such tours. Moreover, regional barriers stand on the way as the linguistic fanaticism is creepy under process. It is, therefore, necessary to expand the vision of such people and create a brand of new stream through a well designed and research-based course and training.

Culturology and Rituology

The rituals have kept alive the spark of Indian culture. All our cultural expressions find their appropriate revelations through rituals embeded in Sanskrit rituological treatises. Since there is a demand to know the scientific aspects of rituals and their importance in day to day life it becomes necessary to provide an applied course which must contribute to the development of cultural and social process.

Futurology

Futurology is one of the time-tested contributions of India. Now this has come out as a new science to formulate predictions as real as possible to plan the future of one's life. This also provides necessary skills for adjustment of one's programme with time through appropriate projections taking the very environmental background into account. What we need is a purposeful course for both teaching and training to improve the futuristic skills that are innate in human mind.

These are some of the ideas normally I put forth on a progressive trend for more considerations. Now Indian society experiences an internal collapse and a frustration in every walk of life. It needs an interruption and a new direction. The only way is to look back and take imperatives from our ancient texts without allowing further negligence.

BIBLIOGRAPHY

1. Bharati A, *et al. Natural Language Processing: A Pāṇinian Perspective*, Prentice-Hall of India Pvt. Ltd., New Delhi, 1995.
2. Dash K.C. (ed), *Sanskrit and Computer*, Pratibha Prakashan, Delhi, 1995.
3. Dash K.C. *Elements of Research Methodology in Sanskrit*, Chukhamba Sanskrit Sansthan, Varanasi, 1992.
4. Nagendra H.R. *Yoga: Its Basis and Application*, Vol. 1, Vivekananda Kendra, Bangalore, 1989.
5. Stall Frits, "The Sanskrit of Sciences", *Journal of Indian Philosophy*, Vol. 23, (pp. 73-127) 1995, Kluwer Academic Publishers, Dordrecht, Netherlands.
6. Behera, N. *Logic of a Simple Form of Sanskrit* (Ph.D. Thesis), Sri Jagannatha Sanskrit Vishvavidyalaya, (Unpublished Ph.D. Thesis) Puri, 1995.
7. Dikshit, S. *Sanskrit in Modern Times*, Sri Jagannatha Sanskrit Vishvavidyalaya, (Unpublished Ph.D. Thesis) , Puri, 1990.

3

REVAMPING INDOLOGICAL RESEARCH : SOME SUGGESTIONS

C. Rajendran

If we are prepared to make some soul searching about the exact state of Indological research in India at present, we will not fail to encounter some pressing problems which demand our serious engagement and corrective measures. Such an exercise may be exasperating; but it is sure to prove to be quite rewarding in the long run. We have to review the progress made hitherto, and take stock of the present position and to think of remedial measures for the major problems facing Indology. The present paper claims to be only an honest attempt at this inevitable venture and it is hoped that it will provoke specialistis, agencies and other organisations into meaningful action.

There cannot be any doubt of the fact that Indological research on modern lines were initiated by European academicians in their attempt to come into terms with the complex realities of India during the colonial days. Of course traditional scholarship was not totally ignorant of methodological problems; in fact no culture can register the progress made as in ancient India without an inbuilt research orientation. But the fact remains that there was a qualitative change in our approach to knowledge with the advent of modern scholarship. Most of the European scholars were multi-linguals trained in various academic disciplines who could handle the abundant data available on truly scientific and systematic manner. Armed physically with the amenities of the Industrial revolution and mentally with the scientific spirit generated by Renaissance, those stalwarts approached Sanskrit, Indian History, religion, philosophy and a host of allied disciplines in a really professional manner. The galaxy of great orientalists who appeared in the horizon of Indological research include names like Sir William Jones, Colebrook,

Max Muller, Whitney, Winternitz, Bopp, De Saussure and a host of others. Their massive programme included preparation of critical editions of important classics, good translations, literary histories, dictionaries and interpretation of texts.[1] A generation of diligent scholars of India like Dr. Bhandarkar trained both in ancient and modern lines joined them. Indological departments were established all over the world in universities. The impressive output of more than two centuries, consisting of monumental works like *'The Sacred Books of the East'*, dictionaries, critical editions and thousands of articles in hundreds of Indological journals speak for themselves about the breath taking pace with which this discipline developed in India and abroad. It even paved the way for new branches of knowledge like comparative philology and comparative religion.

When one surveys the post-Independence scenaries of Indological research, one cannot escape the feeling that the hey-day of Indology seems to be a matter of past. This is not to under rate the importance of the works done by some very gifted and dedicated scholars in various fields. What we really miss is the much awaited take off of Indological studies where tradition and modernity could meet in a meaningful dialogue. Indological studies have actually retreated and withdrawn from the mainstream and whatever work is being done is confined to the fold of the diminishing tribe of Indologists. Sanskrit is taught and studied in isolation and deprived of the opportunity of cross-cultural fertilisation of ideas. The result has been a retradation of the growth of Indological research.

The main reason for this sorry state of affairs is that Sanskrit has not been assigned a definite role in the curriculum in the language policy evolved in the independent India. The result has been disastrous. We are witnessing the emergence of a new generation of intelligentia which is totally ignorant of our past and Indology, confined to specialists and scholars, is deprived of an opportunity to open up new vistas due to the lack of the exposure to mainstream culture.

If we make a random survey of the topics selected for research in Indology in contemporary India, we see a depressing lack of originality and daring search for new avenues. There is seldom an attempt for inter-disciplinary approach to problems. Many scholars are content with descriptive accounts of topics. In literary studies, insights of modern tools like narratology and stylistics are almost never used. Inter-disciplinary approach is eschewed in other various fields like Indian philosophy, grammar, Vedic studies and the like.[2] On the other hand, the generation of historians, linguists, philosophers, literary critics and legal experts proficient in Sanskrit is also fast disappearing with the result that there is a complete break between traditional knowledge and contemporary society.

This sorry state is compounded by the fact that many research projects are duplications of works already done or are undertaken simultaneously in different parts of the country without mutual knowledge. Many universities allow research works being undertaken in languages other than English and there is, theoretically, nothing wrong in it. But in the practical side, a situation has emerged where a Malayali is at a loss to understand what is going on in Karnataka or Bengal with regard to Indological research. This does not augur well for an internationally acclaimed branch of knowledge where one has always to keep pace with the latest orientations and tendencies.

Another serious problem facing a prospective researcher is the non-availability of vital data in the research field. Research digests which give the latest tendencies in a nutshell are conspicuous by their absence. Association of Indian Universities bring periodic compilations of the dissertations accepted for Ph.D. work and journals like *Pracījyoti* give concise accounts of research work. But a comprehensive publication giving details of Indological research going on across the country can alone guide scholars engaged in research properly. Of late there has been a drastic cut in the funds available for conducting national seminars where specialists could get the valuable opportunity for exchanging their ideas.[3] Again it is the research which suffers on account of this.

The following suggestions, if implemented properly would go a long way in restoring Indological research, its lost glory and relevance.

1. Encouraging inter-disciplinary approach in various branches of Indology where the insights of linguistics, anthropology, sociology, philosophy, psychology, political science, historiography, etc., could be pressed into service in the exploration of new avenues and methodology. Such research programmes could be introduced at M. Phil. and Ph.D. levels. If necessary two guides belonging to Sanskrit and modern disciplines may be entrusted with the supervision of the research work. New areas of research will refresh the already stale academic field.

2. If the research work is being done in a regional language, proper care should be taken to see that it is not a duplication of some work already done. Again, the abstract of the work should be made available to the world of researchers in English so that it is acknowledged to the body of knowledge. Outstanding works appearing in regional languages should be made available to the outside world through translations.
3. A uniform methodology and style sheet should be evolved throughout India in research work being undertaken in Universities, colleges and Vidyapithas.[3] For this, the HRD Ministry and bodies like A.I.O.C. could constitute a committee of experts and their guidelines should be meticulously followed in the evaluation of the research work.
4. There should be periodic workshops and orientation programmes for research scholars and teachers throughout the country where new avenues of research could be discussed.
5. A national journal of high standard of Indological studies should be started which could be converted to a stimulating organ for the experts to air their views on Indological problems also.
6. The U.G.C. should be entrusted to evaluate and grade the existing Indological journals so that standard could be maintained throughout the country properly.
7. Vigorous training may be imparted to research scholars in modern disciplines like linguistics so that horizons of research would show considerable expansion.

NOTES

1. I do not argue that the perception generated by these Orientalists about India and her past is completely faultless. The critique of orientalism made by modern scholars like Edwar must definitely be taken into account. This however, does not diminish the historical importance of the Orientalists.
2. There have been some meaningful dialogues between traditional and modern scholars in some areas of logic, philosophy and linguistics. But these are only stray occurrences. Such colloqury should be organised more frequently.
3. The Orientation/Refresher courses arranged for the teachers could be converted into the research programmes to communicate the latest in various fields of Indology.
4. Computer technology should be introduced to aid research. The MCA style sheet can be regarded as a model, but a more specialised methodology has to be formulated for uniform application in Indology.

4

METHODOLOGY IN INDIAN PHILOSOPHICAL RESEARCH

Raghunath Ghosh

I

The methodology of philosophical research, Indian or Western, is almost the same. In this paper an effort has been made to throw some light on the methodology in philosophical research with special reference to India. The Indian philosophical research has a long tradition commencing from the Upaniṣadic time to modern age. The method of research adopted by our *Śāstrakāras* is an ideal one and relevant even in the present time. But unfortunately this methodology is not always taken care of by our modern scholars due to the various reasons which we shall try to explore afterwards. In the first part of my paper an effort will be made to throw some light on the research methodology adopted by our ancient scholars and perfection of the same. The second part of the paper will concentrate on the present status of research in the field of Indian philosophy. In this connection the brighter and darker side of such research will be focussed. Incidentally problems in adopting the proper methodology have been highlighted. In the concluding part some suggestions have been made to develop research in this field.

II

The Indian philosophical system is called *darśana* which indirectly points to a perfect research method.

It is true and the problems are different in different *Darśanas*. But there is a common feature also in all the *Darśanas* in respect of methodology. This common feature may be regarded as a defining feature of *Darśana*. The term literally means 'seeing' which comes from the root *dṛś* i.e., to see. Mere 'seeing' is not *Darśana*. 'Seeing' is of two types: gross (*sthūla*) and subtle (*sūkṣma*). When an object is seen, it is not called *Darśana* on account of the fact that at this stage there is no confirmation of the knowledge of an object seen. Hence, there is necessity of 'subsequent seeing' the object which is already seen. This is called 'critical observation' which is of subtle type. This 'critical seeing or observation' is *Darśana* in the true sense of the term. When we see some thing e.g., the beautiful mountain etc., this is not *Darśana*. But when we critically see the already seen object, (i.e. review the viewed object) it is called *Darśana*. This seeing is to discover the logic behind why it is beautiful, whether it is real or not, the process of the knowledge of the seen object etc. Hence, this is called *Darśana*.

Though the meaning of the term *Darśana* is taken as 'critically seeing' in object presuated to us, yet the meaning of the term can be intended to not only critically seeing but also critically hearing what is told to us or critically thinking etc., about the object which is presented to us. If it is said, 'protect the curd from the crows' (*kākebhyo dadhī rakṣyatām*), it means to protect the curd from other animals also apart from crows. Here, 'the animals other than crows' is taken in a figurative sense. That is, in this case the implicative meaning of the term '*kākebhyaḥ*' ('from the crows') is taken into account.[1] In the same way, the term *Darśana* may mean 'critical thinking', 'critical hearing' etc., by the implicative meaning of the term.

If a theory or concept is given, one should critically think (*manana*) on the theory or the fact already given or one should critically hear what is already presented. This phenomenon of critical hearing is also called *Darśana*.

Further, it can be said that a literature will be treated as 'philosophical' if there is the methodology consisting of *Uddeśa, lakṣaṇa* and *Parīkṣā*.[2] The methods like *Uddeśa* (introduction), *lakṣaṇa* (definition) and *Parīkṣā* (critical examination) of what has been said are essential factors in philosophy. A literature containing *Uddeśa* and *Lakṣaṇa* but not *Parīkṣā*, is not treated as 'philosophical'. In Indian research-methodology the role of *Parīkṣā* or critical examination along with *Uddeśa* and *Lakṣaṇa* is fundamental and hence, it may be described as a defining feature of *Darśana*.

The element of *Parīkṣā* has been taken care of in all the systems of

Indian Philosophy. This phenomenon of 'critical examination' has also been described by Vātsyāyana as '*Anvīkṣā*' in the sense mentioned above. Though Vātsyāyana has coined the term '*Anvīkṣā*' in the context of *Nyāyadarśana* only, it may be true in the case of other *Darśanas* also. Because, all the *Darśanas* in India take recourse to *Anvīkṣā* which means 'critical examination'. The term consists of two words - '*Anu*' (meaning 'after'), *īkṣā* (knowledge). The term *Anvikṣā* means 'subsequent-knowledge' i.e., the critical adjugation of the facts or theories already presented to us. Though the term '*īkṣā* is taken in the sense of knowledge, it will literally mean 'seeing' (*īkṣaṇa*) which is equivalent to *Darśana* (seeing). By the secondary implication the terms '*Ikṣaṇa*' or *Darśana* mean knowing critically about what is known through other means like perception, etc.[3] The prefix '*Anu*' with *īkṣā* indicates that the seeing or knowing critically is *Darśana* or *Anvīkṣā*, but not knowing as it is without any critical thinking. In fact, knowing an object is not complete till it is not confirmed by subsequent critical reasoning. In order to highlight this the prefix '*anu*' is attached to '*īkṣā*. Such a critical reflection is common to all the *Darsanaśāstras*, means of all actions and foundations of all religions.[4] Hence, 'critical reflection' (*Anvīkṣā*) is the only defining feature of *Darśana*. This phenomenon is also known as *Manana* as told earlier. In other words, *Manana* is to be understood as *Darśana* by implication. The critical examination of the theory or statement already presented is called *Manana*.

According to Dharmarāja Adhvarīndra, the phenomenon of *Manana* is a kind of psychic process, which, when in respect of a particular meaning of a word there is doubt as to the conflict with other *pramāṇas*, causes knowledge in the form of *Tarka* which becomes promoter to remove the doubt. That is to say, a scholar tries to examine through his intellect that which he has known from other sources is correct. The method called *Manana* is a stage when an individual applies some argument in favour of his own standpoint or in order to make his position more firm-footed by way of removing the doubt regarding the nature of an object.[5]

This 'examination' also is a kind of subsequent logical investigation. It has been stated that each and every theory is to be examined critically and logically (*Paścānman-tavyastarkataḥ*). The statement or theory which is presented is not to be taken in its face-value until and unless it is confirmed by critical examination.

When a theory is examined, there will be two types of result of the examination. One may completely or partly reject the earlier view or may re-interpret the earlier one. Both may be the result of the critical examination and in both the cases one should forward some logical ground for reinterpreting or rejecting the earlier thesis. Because, a statement whch is not properly grounded cannot impress others. If some standpoint is rejected or reinterpreted, it should be substantiated through argument, because the groundless speech will fall flat upon others and hence, it cannot substantiate one's own philosophical position.[6]

In philosophical research each and every position is subject to challenge and hence, no position is every final. The whole Indian philosophical position is developed on the basis of *Pūrvapakṣa-uttarapakṣa*-debate. That which is accepted as a *Siddhāntapakṣa* by a particular school is critically examined and rejected by another school. Hence, that which is a *siddhāntapakṣa* may become *pūrvapakṣa* in the eyes of another philosopher afterwards. All philosophical conclusions are *prima facie* in character. Had they been final, it would have to be presumed that no question should be asked regarding this. If so, there would be no philosophical growth and development, which is not desirable. This research method makes the philosophical tradition alive after removing intellectual inertia. In this way the philosophical research proceeds. Even in the case of reinterpretation of some views, some philosophical problems are generally raised in accepting certain views and probable solutions have been offered. Though there is the refutation of the view, there is a fresh interpretation which follows from the original theory. This is also a kind of research which gives a justification of the mother-theory. Mostly the commentarial literature (*ṭīkā, vārttika, bhāṣya* etc.) develops by way of justifying the original text. At the time of justification or clarification the *Bhāṣyakāras* or *ṭīkākāras* raise various problems which could be raised by the opponents and give a solution of them in order to defend the original view. The commentators presuppose what opponent might say against their philosophical stand and hence they incline to offer a solution of the problems. This methodology is adopted in almost all the philosophical literature in India including poetic, literary criticism etc.

In order to indicate that theories propounded are the result of intensive research where the determination of truth is the main objective, but there is no question of victory in the debate, all the philosophers have described their theories as *Vāda* e.g. *nirvikalpavāda, jagatkāraṇatāvāda, avayavavāda, satkāryavāda* etc. In the case of *Vāda* category of debate the scholar substantiates his own standpoint and refutes other's view with the help of *Pramāṇa, Tarka, Pañcāvayava* etc.[7] This is the proper methodology of research adopted in India.

III

Let us see the present status of research found in the Indian philosophical world. The methodology which was taken as paradigm is still followed by a section of scholars who either rejects or reinterprets the earlier thesis through reasoning. Sometimes inter-disciplinary research is also conducted or in progress on some areas, which gives us a broader perspective of a problem. Apart from this a section of scholars is trying to open a dialogue between East and West after making a comparative study, which can be taken as a healthy step on account of the fact that the Indian philosophical themes can be presented to scholars conversant with Western philosophy. The culture or society or presupposition under which a particular philosophical system is built up is different in different cases and hence, it is not always possible or justifiable to make a comparative estimate. In spite of this a comparative study sometimes gives an idea about what is going on within different systems of Indian philosophy and within Indian and Western philosophy. In the present day unfortunately it is found that a few scholars are not adhering to this research methodology. They simply quote what others have said on the particular theory which does not bear any mark of critical thinking. It is also found that a few scholars are doing philosophical research on Indian Classical philosophical texts without going through the original Sanskrit texts, which is not desirable. The research work based on the secondary sources like English or Hindi translation cannot do justice to the subject. One is inclined to go through secondary sources primarily to get rid of Sanskrit language and terminology. Without the knowledge of Sanskrit language and terminology one cannot do what is called 'research' in the true sense of the term in Indian Philosophy.

It may be argued following Jayanta Bhaṭṭa that the whole Indian philosophical literature is as vast as Ocean and hence there is hardly any new thing which we could find (*Kuto vā nutanaṁ vastu vayamutprekṣituṁ kṣamāḥ*[8]). It is true that there is nothing in Indian Philosophy which is untold so far. Hence, though there is no novelty in theories or thought, there may be novelty in presentation or reinterpretation (*vacovinyāsamātraṁ*)[9] for which the proper understanding of the intricacies of the technical Sanskrit terms is essential.

IV

For promoting proper research in the field of Indian philosophy in the present day the following suggestions can be made.

First, Sanskrit teaching and Sanskrit learning should be encouraged among the present generation. Only learning Sanskrit language cannot solve all the problems. Because, the technique or methodology of presenting a theory developed after 10th century (just after the emergence of Navya Nyāya) has become highly technical. The Navya Nyāya language becomes an ideal of intellectual expression in this age. Hence, we find the treatises on Vedānta like *Advaitasiddhi, Vedāntaparibhāṣā, Śikhāmaṇi* and *Maṇiprabhā* on *Vedāntaparibhāṣā* etc. which are based on Navya Nyāya language. Even texts on poetics like *Rasagaṅgādhara* by Jagannath Pandita are written in the same fashion. Unless one masters over the language, the mere knowledge of Sanskrit does not help much. If someone masters over the technical language, the reward is an intellectual satisfaction. One cannot have mastery over this if one is not undergone through proper training under the guidance of an able *Guru*, which is possible only in traditional way of learning in the *tols* or *pāṭhaśālās*. For the proper research in Indian philosophy there should be some facilities of learning in a traditional way so that modern scholars may come in contact with the traditional *paṇḍits* and discuss problems with them after going out of the technicalities. Hence, Sanskrit should be introduced in each and every academic institution where the research in different fields is being conducted.

Secondly, it is essential to represent the Indian philosophical literature in the terminology adopted in the West so that others trained in Western logic can enjoy the logical excellence of India within knowing much Sanskrit. Some of the modern thinkers like Professor B.K. Motilal, Professor J.N. Mohanty, Dr. D.C. Guha, Professor Shibjivan Bhattacharyya etc. had undertaken this job and they had successfully interpreted the Indian philosophical texts in modern Western terminology and sometimes translated into symbolic language. In this way a dialogue can be opened between two traditions, East and West.

Thirdly, the reading of Sanskrit texts, mastering over terminology, and critical estimate of what is already given require a Herculian labour of a scholar. One can afford to this if one is provided with financial support for meting the expenditure of research and maintaining himself and his family. If research is meant for getting a degree any how and suitable job, a scholar's primary attention would be to get a degree and a job by hook or crook which makes the research secondary. If some one is given financial stability, he may perform the job of research in a 'free' mind rather seriously. There are some institutions in India where competent persons are appointed for this purpose of research but this should be done in all academic institutions in large scale.

Lastly, there are many important treatises in Sanskrit literature which are either partially or completely lost. Some of them are still available in the manuscripts. For doing justice to the indological research as a whole these lost treasures are to be restored and manuscripts are to be properly edited and published.

REFERENCES

1. Jahadajahallakṣaṇodhāharanaṇtu kākebhyo dadhi rakṣyatāmityādikameva. Tatra śakyakākatvaparityā- genāśakyadadhyupaghātakatvapuraskāreṇa 'kāke ca kākaśabdasya pravṛtteḥ.
   Vedāntaparibhāṣa (Āgamaparicched a).
2. *Nyāyamañjarī*, Āhnika I.
3. "Pratyakṣāgamābhymikṣitasyānvīkṣaṇamanvīkṣā."
   Vātsyāyanabhāṣya on Sūtra 1.1.1.
4. "Pradīpaḥ sarvavidyānāmupāyaḥ sarvakarmaṇām/Āśrayaḥ sarvadharmāṇāṁ vidyoddeśe prakīrttitā//." Ibid.
5. "Mananaṁ nāma śabdāvadhārite' arthe mānāntaraviro-dhaśaṁkāyāṁ tannirākaraṇānukūla-tarkātmakajñānajanako mānasavyāpāraḥ"
   Vedāntaparibhāṣā, (Viṣayaparicched a)
6. "Aśiraska vacanopanyāse sādhyāsiddheḥ, Ekākinī prātijñā hi pratijñātaṁ na sādhayet."
   Bauddhadarśana,
7. Pramāṇatarka-sādhanopālambhaḥ pakṣapratipakṣa-parigraho vādaḥ" 1.2.42.
8. Jayantabhaṭṭa, *Nyāyamañjarī*, Introduction.
9. Ibid.

5

MORE THAN THREE DECADES OF THE STUDIES OF DHARMAŚĀSTRA

S.G. Moghe

Dr. P.V. Kane completed the last volume of his *History of Dharmaśāstra* (Vol. V. Part II) in the year 1962. Thereafter he also revised the first Volume which ultimately resulted into two volumes. These two volumes are published by the Bhandarkar Oriental Research Institute in the years 1968 and 1975.

About the importance of the voluminous work of MM. Dr. Kane, Jan Gonda of Utrecht, remarks that it is a gigantic - encyclopaedia. He further adds that they contain innumerable extracts from original sources, quotations from hundreds of texts, references to inscriptions and legislative enactments, thought-provoking theories, sharp observations and conscientious judgements. These erudite surveys of the whole field of Dharmaśāstra, this gigantic encyclopaedia that embraces far more than the Śāstra itself, will no doubt prove to be an indispensable tool of many generations of scholars in times to come'.

In the light of this observation, it is necessary to take a survey of the work done during the last three decades and more. It is also necessary to see how far the views and chronological dates proposed by Dr. Kane received modification, addition and corrections. As this subject is very vast, it will not be possible for any scholar to do complete justice to this subject. However, I am tempted to do some justice to this topic, knowing full well my own limitations in this field. I do not claim that I have approach to all the books and journals published all over the world on this subject. But whatever works could become available to me in the course of the last thirty years and more, will be found best utilised for the purpose of this paper.

Incidentally, however, it should be noted that so far as the work on this subject is done in the foreign countries, my source is the *Journal of the Bhandarkar Oriental Research Institute*, and particularly the reviews that have appeared there.

In all humility, I mention here the important work *'Bibliography on Dharma and Artha'* published by Ludwik Sternbach, many years ago, though I have no approach to all the books and articles mentioned in that important work.

I must also mention in this very context, that in the year 1974, I wrote an article on the contribution of MM. Dr. P.V. Kane to the domain of Dharmaśāstra (pp. 65-82) to MM. Dr. P.V. Kane commemoration Monograph published by the University of Bombay in the year 1974. This article has also appeared in my book *'Studies in the Dharmaśāstra'* published in the year 1991.

Now I propose to discuss in this paper a new matter which has not appeared in my article of 1974.

For the proper study of Dharmaśāstra, Dr. Kane has laid down the pattern of the restoration of the lost texts of Dharmaśāstra, by collecting together the citations of that work from the Dharmaśāstra works. He has restored the text[1] of *Śaṅkha-Likhita-Dharma-Sūtra* in the *Annals of the Bhandarkar Oriental Research Institute*. He has also restored the text of the *Kātyāyana Smṛti-Sāroddhāra* by himself publishing this work. This has certainly influenced the later writers on Dharmaśāstra. In this very context, it should be noted that I have also restored[2] only after editing the *Vyāghra-Smṛti* with the help of two manuscripts, the portion from the *Vyāghra-Smṛti* covering 142 stanzas from pp. 108-126 which is actually Appendix II to my edition of the *Vyāghra-Smṛti* published by the authorities of the Bhandarkar Oriental Research Institute. (2) I have also restored the *Ṛṣyaśṛṅga-Smṛti* in the Mysore Orientalist Vol. XIV, pp. 65-77 and this has also appeared in my *'Studies in the Dharmaśāstra*, pp. 65-80. Here I have collected about 73 stanzas on the name of *Ṛṣyaśṛṅga* and have thrown light on his novel view[3] in the Dharmaśāstra. (3) The text of Pulastya is also restored by Lallanji Gopal and Krishna Kanti Gopal and published in Varanasi in the year 1992, as is further clear from the review of this work at the hands of Prof. M.L. Wadekar in the *Journal of the Oriental Institute*, Vol. XL, March-June 1991, pp. 337-340. (4) It is also heard from the reliable sources that the restoration of the Devala Smṛti is done from Baroda by Prof. Wadekar for the Ph.D. Degree in Sanskrit and it is published by Agama Kala Prakashan Delhi, in two volumes. This short survey on the point of restoration of the lost Dharmaśāstra texts bears testimony to the fact that whatever model is laid down by Dr. Kane is followed verbatim by the later scholars.

In the domain of Dharmaśāstra, editing of the manuscripts also forms the basis of further research. Dr. Kane himself has edited the text of the *Vyavahāra Mayūkha* published by the Bhandarkar Oriental Research Institute in the year 1925 and *Madana Ratna-Pradīpa* for the Anup Sanskrit Library, Bikaner, in the year 1948. It should be noted here that in Appendix 'E' to his edition of the *Vyavahāra Mayūkha,* Dr. Kane has quoted the passages where Nīlakaṇṭha has expressly quoted Madana-Ratna and either followed or not criticized. (pp. 513- 515). This kind of editing of the Dharmaśāstra texts has largely influenced the scholars both oriental and occidental. Here a reference could be made to the article of Dr. J.D.M. Derrett who edited the rare manuscript on Dharmaśāstra particularly during the early regime of British India. This manuscript[5] entitled *'Śvaśrū-snuṣā-Dhana- Saṁvāda* is edited by him for Dr. V. Raghavan felicitation and the translation of this manuscript is also published by him in MM. Dr. Umesh Mishra Commemoration Volume brought out by the Ganganath Jha Research Institute, Allahabad, in the year 1970. (2) Miss. J.H. Dave took ample labours for editing the text of *'Śrāddha-Prakāśa of Pṛthīcandra,* a Ph.D. thesis (in an unpublished form) for the University of Bombay, in the year 1959 and particularly guided by Prof. H.D. Velankar. It should be noted here that this thesis is deposited in the library of the University of Bombay. (3) The writer of this note i.e. Dr. Moghe has also edited *'The Buddha Smṛti'* with the help of six manuscripts (two from B.O.R.I., Poona, 1 from Benares, 1 from Adyar Library, Madras, 1 from Oriental Institute, Baroda, and 1 from the India Office Catalogue as noted by Dr. Kane) for the journal of *the Annals of the Bhandarkar Oriental Research. Institute,* Vol. LXIV 1983-pp. 259-268. It may be noted here that Dr. Moghe has further published the manuscript of the *Vyāghra Smṛti* on behalf of the Bhandarkar Oriental Research Institute, Pune, in 1985. Here one manuscript is the one already published by Mansukhalal Mor in the fourth Volume of the *Smṛti-Sandarbha* and particularly the manuscript from the Benaras.

Dr. Moghe also used the manuscript of the Bhandarkar Oriental Research Institute and edited the text with the help of these two manuscripts and also identified the quotations of the *Vyāghra Smṛti* in the light of the vast Dharmaśāstra literature. In addition to this, he has also collected about 142 stanzas on the name of Vyāghra particularly given by the writers on Dharma-Śāstra. (5) Dr. Moghe has also published the critical edition of the *Śrāddha-Sāgara* of Kullūkabhaṭṭa, on the basis of a solitary manuscript from the Sanskrit College, Calcutta. This work is published in the year 1994 by D.K. Printworld (p) Ltd., Delhi. A very good introduction covering 68 printed pages is added to this work by Dr. Moghe, discussing several problems connected with the *Śrāddha- Sāgara* of Kullūkabhaṭṭa. (6) The *Divyatattva* of Raghunandana is published by Richard W. Lariviere, with the help of 50 manuscripts, and this is also reviewed by Dr. G.V. Devasthali in the *Journal of the A.B.O.R.I.* Vol. LXIV-1983-pp. 272-274. The other important publication in this respect is that of the *Nārada- Smṛti* with English Translation and Notes by the American scholar Richard Lariviere. (7) The manuscript entitled *'Dāyabhāga-Vyavasthā-Saṁkṣepa* is edited by Ludo Rocher for Dr. R.N. Dandekar felicitation Volume 1984, pp. 351-358. and (8) Lastly the important manuscript of the *Śrāddha-Pradīpa* of Vipramiśra is published by Dr. Braja Kishore Swain in 1982 with his own commentary in Sanskrit entitled '*Raśmi*'. This book is also reviewed by Dr. Moghe for the *Journal of the A.B.O.R.I. Vol. IXIX* pp 298-301 (1988) and Dr. P.D. Navathe (p. 304). This important survey would reveal that both qualitatively and quantitatively remarkable progress is noticed in respect of editing the rare manuscripts of Dharmaśāstra.

In the domain of research, deciding the chronological dates of the authors and works on Dharmaśāstra plays very important part. Some of the dates fixed by Dr. Kane are challenged and new dates are suggested for same authors. Here a short survey would be necessary. (1) Dr. Kane has placed Kullūkabhaṭṭa, the commentator of the *Manu- Smṛti* between 1150 to 1300 A.D. Dr. Moghe has, however, placed him between 1520-1620 A.D. For the discussion on this aspect, attention may be drawn to paper of Dr. Moghe on the *Date of Kullūkabhaṭṭa* published in *Studies in the Dharmaśāstra*, pp. 103-113. (2) As regards the date of Govindaswāmī, the commentator of the *Baudhāyana Dharma-Sūtra*, the two scholars- Dr. Burnell and Dr. Kane differ. Dr. Burnell treat him to be a modern commentator, while Dr. Kane takes him to be a very late writer. Dr. Moghe has placed him between 1650 to 1690 A.D. and has thus treated him to be a medieval writer. For the discussion on this point, attention is drawn to the discussion in the *Studies in the Dharmaśāstra*, pp. 114-117. (3) As regards the *Buddha-Smṛti*, Dr. Kane has not expressed a definite view. Dr. Kane has fixed the general period of the Smṛti literature. Dr. Moghe has placed him between 10th and 11th century A.D., in a paper published in the A.B.O.R.I. Vol. LXIV- 1983 pp. 259-268. (4) For the date of the *Vyāghra Smṛti*, there is no place in Dr. Kane's *History of Dharmaśāstra*. Dr. Moghe has placed him in the 10th century A.D., particularly in his introduction[7] to the *Vyāghra Smṛti* published by the Bhandarkar Oriental Research Institute in the year 1985. (5) On the date of Ṛṣyaśṛṅga-Smṛti, Dr. Kane is silent in his work. Dr. Moghe has, however, placed him in the tenth or eleventh century A.D. particularly in a paper[8] *'Ṛṣyaśṛṅga Smṛti-restored'* contributed to Mysore Orientalist. (6) As regards the date of Vaidyanātha Dīkṣita, it must be stated that Dr. Kane has placed him in the 17th century. However, the writer of this note has placed him between 1700 and 1750 A.D. by a paper[9] on 'Vaidyanātha Dīkṣita' contributed to the *Journal of the Asiatic Society*, Bombay, Volumes 60-61 for 1985 and 1986, pp. 56-61.

Interpretation of Dharmaśāstra texts also becomes an interesting topic of research. In interpreting the text, it would be worthy of note to mention some differences with the views of Dr. Kane. (1) In interpreting the famous line from the *Manu- Smṛti 'Nakṣatraiḥ yaśca jīvati'* III. 162, Dr. Kane takes this as a reference to the professional astrologer who should not be invited for a lunch at the *Śrāddha* ceremony. Dr. Moghe differs from Dr. Kane and points out that this has a reference to the same astrologer who does not possess the proper knowledge of astrology and goes on foretelling the fortunes of the people. This paper[10] is contributed to the *Journal of the Bharatiya Vidya*, Bombay. (2) In the case of famous Śunaḥśepa, Dr. Kane treats him as a *datrima* son, relying upon the authority of the *Vasiṣṭha Dharma-Sūtra*. Dr. Moghe simply points out in a paper[11] contributed to the *Journal of the Ganganatha Jha Kendriya Sanskrit Vidyapitha*, that Śunaḥśepa belongs to the category of a *Kṛtrima* son of Viśvāmitra, if at all the authority of the text of *Aitareya Brāhmaṇa* is respected. He has also shown that in the history of adoption, the case of Śunaḥśepa is, indeed, a unique case. (3) Dr. Kane has not at all considered the interpretation of the Dharmaśāstra texts at the hands of non-Dharmaśāstra authors like Abhinavagupta. Dr. Moghe has properly considered[12] the interpretation of the text of the *Gautama Dharma Sūtra* IX. 35 by Abhinavagupta, particularly in comparison with the interpretations of the regular commentators - Haradatta and Maskari and has demonstrated that the interpretation offered by Abhinavagupta is, no doubt, novel; but it suffers from the fault of *Parisaṁkhyā*, well-known in the science of Pūrva-Mīmāṁsā. This paper is accepted for publication by the research journal of G.J.K.S.V, Allahabad. Incidentally, it may be added here that this paper has found a place in the present author's *Studies in the Dharmaśāstra*, pp. 172-177. (4) Dr. Moghe has followed by the view point of Dr. Kane in interpreting[13] the *Kauṭilya Arthaśāstra* III. 5.28, by suggesting that the word *strī* occurring in the *Kauṭilya Arthaśāstra* has a reference to a kept woman on a concubine who is entitled to the property of a person and not to a wife as held by others. This paper is published in the *Journal of the Oriental Institute*, Baroda. (5) For the interpretation of the interesting passages from the *Kauṭilya Arthaśāstra*, the attention of the readers is drawn to the present author's book '*Studies in the Dharmaśāstra*' pp. 220-270. All these papers have already appeared in the research journals and they are brought together in the above book.

In the field of research, it is equally important to know whether there is any real progress in understanding the significance of some concepts or some technical terms that occur in the body of the texts of Dharmaśāstra. (1) In appreciating the significance of the expression '*ananyapūrvikām* in the *Yājñavalkya-smṛti* I. 51, the regular commentators of the *Yājñavalkya-smṛti* have simply given faithful rendering of the expression. Dr. Moghe has shown the significance of this expression in the light of the *Mahābhārata* evidence with reference to Ambā and Śiśupāla, particularly by applying the rules of the Dharmaśāstra texts. This paper is published in the present author's *Studies in the Dharmaśāstra*, pp. 159-164. (2) The concept of Nyāsa is fully explained by Dr. Kane in his *History of Dharmaśāstra*, Vol. III. But Dr. Moghe has shown how this concept of Nyāsa has undergone evolution[15] in the Classical Sanskrit literature, even including the evidence from the *Rāmāyaṇa* and the *Mahābhārata*. This is shown by him in a paper contributed to the *Journal of the Oriental Institute*, Tirupati, and has found its proper place in the present author's book '*A Peep at Indology*' pp. 35-42. (3) In appreciating the sense of the word

'Bhrūṇa' in the Dharmaśāstra, Dr. Kane has done justice from the point of view of Dharmaśāstra texts. But he has failed to consider the evidence from the *Rāmāyaṇa* and the *Mahābhārata*. Even in the modern Sanskrit lexicon prepared by V.S. Apte and revised by P.K. Gode and others, the meanings given by Dr. Moghe in the light of the above evidence have no place at all. In this article[16] *'Dharmaśāstra Aspects of the Rāmāyaṇa'* which is awaiting publication from the research journal but which has a place in the present author's book *' A Peep at Indology'* pp. 31-32 may be consulted by the serious readers of Dharmaśāstra. (4) In appreciating the concept of a witness, Dr. Kane has done some justice. But Dr. Moghe has considered this concept[17] in the light of the *Mahābhārata* and Dharmaśāstra literature in his book *'A Peep at Indology'* pp. 19-22. It may be added in passing that this paper is also accepted by the authorities of the Oriental Journal, Tirupati, for publication. (5) As regards the concept of *'Sāpiṇḍya'* i.e. consanguinity, there is a lot of discussion in Kane's *History of Dharmaśāstra*. The generally accepted view is that *Sāpiṇḍya* is accepted upto 5th degree on mother's side and seventh degree on the side of father. But *Buddhasmṛti* edited by the present author for the *Annals of the Bhandarkar Oriental Journal* for 1983, holds a different view. Buddha accepts *Sāpiṇḍya* upto the tenth degree on father's side. It is further interesting to note that one finds corroboration to this view in the commentary *'Keśava- Vaijayantī'* by Nandapaṇḍita on the *Viṣṇu-Smṛti*, published by the Adyar Library, Madras. It may be noted in passing that this Nandapaṇḍita belongs to the 17th century A.D. This important view[18] of Buddha has just escaped the view of Dr. Kane and this has been pointed out by the present writer. (6) Dr. J.D.M. Derrett has placed his unerring finger on *'An Aspect of the Arranged Marriage in Dharmaśāstra'* in his article contributed to the Diamond Jubilee Volume of the *Annals of the Bhandarkar Oriental Research Institute* published in the year 1978. Here the article covers the pp. 107- 120. This aspect has escaped the notice of Dr. Kane. (7) In Dr. Kane's work, one does not find the clarification of the term *'Svayaṁpāka'* used in the context of the *Śrāddha* ceremony. Here the attention may be drawn to the significant explanation[19] of Vyāghra who says that when the food for the *Śrāddha* ceremony is cooked either by the *Yajamāna* himself, or by his wife or by his son, then that cooked food is called as *Svayaṁpāka'*. Dr. Kane has not touched one important point in respect of the *Śrāddha,* ceremony. The question often arises as to whether

some persons are treated as disqualified from preparing or cooking the *Śrāddha* food. Dr. Kane has not touched this point. Here it may be pointed that according to Vyāghra, the food for the *Śrāddha* ceremony is not to be prepared by a daughter, a widow, a childless woman, a pregnant woman and a woman with bad appearance. It seems that Dr. Kane could not use this view of Vyāghra for the simple reason that at the time of his writing the volumes of *History of Dharma-śāstra*, the *Vyāghra Smṛti* was not critically edited by any scholar. (8) The concept of a widow needs some explanation. Generally it is an accepted view that when a husband is dead, his wife is treated as widow. But in the Dharmaśāstra literature, Kane has not taken any note[20] of the *Kapila Smṛti*. This Smṛtikāra holds that a woman is treated as a widow when she has no husband and son alive. This means that when she has a son alive, she is not to be treated as a widow. This revolutionary view of *Kapila-Smṛti* has not attracted the mind of Dr. Kane, for the simple reason that this was published later in the volumes of the *Smṛti-Sandharbha* by Mansukhalal from Calcutta. (9) In Dr. Kane's work, one does not find adequate information in respect of the persons to whom the duaghters may not be given in marriage. This aspect has escaped the eagle eye of Dr. Kane. Hemādri quotes on the *Raghuvaṁśa* VI. 23 a stanza[21] from the text of *Vṛddha-Parāśara*. This stanza means that those persons who are always away from home, who are not educated, who have concentrated their mind on getting emancipation, who are brave and who are pauper, should not be given their daughters in marriage by the house-holders.

The readers of Dharmaśāstra know very well that Dr. Kane has written special chapters in the fifth volume of the *History of Dharmaśāstra* on the relation of the Dharmaśāstra to Sāṁkhya, Yoga, Tarka, Purāṇas and Pūrva-Mīmāṁsā. But he has not touched the other topics like Dharmaśāstra[22] and *Gṛhyasūtras*, Dharmaśāstra[23] and Kāmaśāstra, Dharmaśāstra[24] and Āyurveda, and Dharmaśāstra[25] and Sanskrit lexicons. Some of these topics are discussed by the writer of this note in the Journals and they are brought together in the *Studies in the Dharmaśāstra*. Here it must be clarified that though Dr. Kane has not written chapters on these topics, he has utilised the matter in these works for the *History of Dharmaśāstra*. So it can be said with reasonable certainty that some of the gaps in the work of Dr. Kane are filled in by the writer of this note, though it is true that his work cannot come up to the level of Dr. Kane. Here incidentally, it may be added that Dr. Derrett finds fault with Dr. Kane's work, for not having consulted the sources of Sociology and Anthropology, in his *History of Dharmaśāstra*. In passing, it may also be added that a small gap[26] in the work of Dr. Kane, is filled in by considering the experience from the Classical Sanskrit literature by connecting it with the *History of Dharmaśāstra* thoughts. This work has been done by Dr. A.N. Deo for his Ph.D. thesis (now deposited in the library of the Marathwada University) and particularly guided by the writer of this note. It can be said categorically that from the works of the 13th century upto the 19th century, a prospective researcher may consult particularly the classical Sanskrit literature from the point of view of Dharmaśāstra thought. But this is the topic we reserve for some future scholar.

Some interesting points on the total neglect of Dr. Kane deserve mention. Though it is universally admitted that Dr. Kane's work is a voluminous work, some remaining work aims to be done. Right at the out set it must be pointed out that owing to old age, the topics of the digest works of Vaidyanātha Dīkṣita and Vaidika Sārva-bhauma have escaped the eagle eye of Dr. Kane. The present author has contributed an article[27] on Vaidyanātha Dīkṣita to the *Journal of the Asiatic Society* of Bombay and has thus filled up the gap. The work of Vaidika Sārvabhauma deserves treatment. Besides, it will be admitted by any serious reader of Dharmaśāstra that some of the Smṛti works have received only a partial treatment at the hands of Dr. Kane. Some such Smṛti works should be restored by the future research scholars. I make the mention of some such Smṛti[28] works only in the foot-note. Unless such Smṛtis are properly restored, nothing can be said about their contribution to the Dharmaśāstra thoughts. In addition to this, Mansukhalal Mor from Calcutta has published in 6 volumes some Smṛtis. There is not a single chapter on these Smṛtis in the *History of Dharmaśāstra*. Hence the writer of this note takes this oppertunity to request or appeal to the interested scholars of the Dharmaśāstra to undertake this kind of work on a grand scale. I prefer to mention[29] some such Smṛtis in the foot-note on which some work deserves to be done.

The importance of the manuscripts in writing the history of any subject is supreme. It must be stated here without any fear of contradiction that though Dr. Kane has consulted some descriptive catalogues of the manuscripts for his monumental history of

Dharmaśāstra and for his section on the *Buddha-Smṛti* alias *Buddha Dharma-Sūtra*. Dr. Kane refers to the two manuscripts on the *Budha Smṛti* in the Bhandarkar Oriental Research Institute, particularly on page 287. It must be stated here that in the list of the works on Dharmaśāstra, Dr. Kane makes a reference to the manuscript of the *Budha Smṛti* printed in India Office Catalogue Vol. III p. 386 (No. 1323) particularly on Page No. 1078. But when the present writer edited this manuscript for the *Annals of the Bhandarkar Oriental Research Institute*, for 1983, he found some additional manuscripts which are not at all mentioned by Dr. Kane. Thus, he could secure the manuscript No. TR 690 at the Adyar Library and Research Centre, Madras. One more manuscript he could get from the Oriental Institute, Baroda. He could also succeed in getting one more manuscript printed in the *Smṛti-Sandharbha* Vol. IV. pp. 2137-2138 particularly from the Royal Asiatic Society of Calcutta. It should be remarked here that in the list of the works on Dharmaśāstra, prepared by that great scholar, there is no mention of any manuscript on the *Vyāghra Smṛti* (p. 1113). But the present author found one manuscript of the *Vyāghra Smṛti* in the Bhandarkar Oriental Research Institute, Pune, bearing No. 163 of 1884-86. In addition to this, he found that the manuscript of the *Vyāghta-smṛti* is published in the *Smṛtisandharbha* Vol. IV. pp. 2491- 2528. This manuscript is, however, printed in the volume of the *Smṛtisandarbha* by procuring the same from the Govt. Sanskrit College, Benares.

I am happy to mention here that for critically editing the *Vyāghra Smṛti*, he made the best use of both the manuscripts. These two illustrations cited above are sufficient to prove my finding that in the matter of editing any manuscript of Dharmaśāstra, the matter presented by Dr. Kane is insufficient. One thus feels that the importance of the *Catalogus Catalogorum* prepared by Dr. V. Raghavan and others from Madras, is indeed, supreme. Every cautious worker on Indology is expected to make the best use of such catalogues for doing the methodical work. Here, incidentally, it may be noted that Dr. Kane also has not made a claim that he has consulted all the catalogues for the purpose of his volumes. Hence there is no point in blaming him as such. I have only casually cited the above illustrations to caution the future readers of Indology and particularly the interested readers of Dharmaśāstra. (3) The importance of the manuscript is also supreme for filling up the gaps in the previously pointed texts. This point has already been clarified by the present author by contributing a paper[30] on *'Nīlakaṇṭha's Vyavahāra Mayūkha* and *Śvaśrū-Snuṣā-Dhana-Saṁvāda'* to the *Journal of the Asiatic Society of Bombay*. Here in passing, it should be noted that the anonymous Śāstrī who wrote the above manuscript supplied some matter which is missing on page 139 of the critical edition of the *Vyavahāra Mayūkha* so ably brought out by MM. Dr. P.V. Kane. This manuscript presents some new readings which have no place in the *Critical Edition of the Vyavahāra Mayūkha*. Besides, if the portion so supplied by the manuscript is added in the matter of page 139 of the *Vyavahāra Mayūkha*, one gets the important observation of Nīlakaṇṭha that he is rejecting the view point of Madana-ratna. In this way, the importance of the manuscript can be very well stressed. This manuscript is also recorded by Dr. Kane in his *History of Dharmaśāstra* Vol. I/II p. 1131. In passing, recently interested scholars of Dharmaśāstra are taking pains to publish some rare manuscripts in the Journals. Casually, I would mention a few such cases in the foot-notes to this article.

The next important point is whether the suggsations made by Dr. Kane for the codification of the Hindu law are accepted by the modern legislature or not. (1) During the British regime, the Hindu law was based on the Dharmaśāstra texts of Manu, Yājñavalkya, Nīlakaṇṭha and others. Dr. Kane made the suggestion that the Hindu law should be codified in view of the changing circumstances as a result of which the importance of the Dharmaśāstra texts was decreased. This suggestion of Dr. Kane was favoured by the modern legislature. In this respect, the role of Dr. Kane in the Rājyasabhā of the nation, is indeed noteworthy. (2) For the Hindu Adoptions and Maintenance Act, Dr. Kane made the vital suggestion in respect of the age of the boy to be adopted. Dr. Kane states that no boy is to be adopted after the age of 5 years. If at all, he is to be adopted, he must be adopted before the *saṁskāra* known as *cūḍā-karma* is performed on him. But it is evident from the provision of the section 10(4) of the Hindu Adoptions and Maintenance Act that the boy or a girl should not have completed the age of 15. If it is borne in mind, one would realise that Dr. Kane's suggestion in respect of the age is turned down by the modern legislature. Besides, Dr. Kane's suggestion that no one can be adopted after the *Upanayana* ceremony is performed on a boy, is not favoured[31] by the modern legislature. (3) Dr. Kane's further suggestion that no one can be adopted after his marriage in the natural family, is also set at naught by the Provision of the section (10) (iii) of the Hindu Adoptions and Maintenance Act of 1956.The modern legislature further held that if a custom in a perticular community permits the adoption of the married person, then there is nothing wrong in it. (4) The modern legislature also has not accepted the Mīmāṁsā principle of *Adṛṣṭa* accepted by the ancient Smṛtikāras, commentators and digest authors. In a case of Madhavarao Vs. Raghunatharao particularly argued by Dr. Kane on the basis of the Mīmāṁsā principle of *Adṛṣṭa* and *sagotra* marriages, relying on the Mitākṣarā arguments, are not accepted[32] by Justice P.B. Gajendragadkar. All these points are already noted by the writer of this note in the research journals. (5) Dr. Kane has made a vital suggestion[33] for the chapter of the *Strīdhana* of the Hindu Law. He recommends that woman's sons and daughters should succeed together. *Strīdhana* should be the absolute property of the married lady and the husband should succeed to the estate of a married lady, when there are no heirs. This suggestion is made by the learned doctor in his *History of Dharmaśāstra*, Vol. III pp. 801- 802. Fortunately this suggestion of the learned doctor is accepted by the modern legislature.

It would be interesting to note the differences with the views of Dr. Kane what he has maintained in his *History of Dharmaśāstra*. (1) Dr. Kane has shown that in the matter of sacrifices, a woman is given a subordinate position, that she is not entitled to perform a sacrifice as such. For such views, he has relied on the *Manu-Smṛti* Vol. 155, *Viṣṇu-Dharma-Sūtra* 25.15 and *Āpastamba Dharma-Sūtra* II.6.15.17. Dr. Moghe begs to differ from Dr. Kane on the basis of the weighty historical evidence, Anantadeva's Mīmāṁsā interpretation and Śabara's important observations, and the views of MM. Ganganatha Jha on the *Mīmāṁsā Sūtra* VI. 1.13 and thinks that women are entitled to perform sacrifices. (2) As regards the three dates of donation, Dr. Kane has clarified his position relying on *Mitākṣarā* on the *Yajñavalkya-Smṛti* I. 203. Here Dr. Moghe has combined[35] the sources of the *Rāmāyaṇa* and the *Mahābhārata*, and has suggested a somewhat different rates of the donation in his article on '*Dāna* section of the Dharmaśāstra (based on the *Mahābhārata*). (3) Dr. Kane thinks that in the *Manuśmṛti* III. 162, the professional Astrologer is prohibited for the lunch at the *Śrāddha*. Dr. Moghe departs[36] from Dr. Kane and holds on the basis of the evidences from the Dharmaśāstra and Astrology that a same astrologer is condemned by Manu for the *Śrāddha*-Ceremony. *(4)* In *Ṛṣi-Kalpanyāsa*, Dr. Kane holds[37] that it is not obligatory on women to apply Tilaka mark on the forehead. It is difficult to agree with the learned scholars on this point. One can quote here the stanza[38] No. 192 (of my critical edition) of the *Vyāghra Smṛti* which clearly means that a brahmin without a *tilaka* mark on his forehead and a pious lady without having the *tilaka* mark of saffron on her forehead, these two are condemned among the people and particularly in respect of the matters - *Daiva* and *Pitrya*. This point is already raised by me in my introduction to the *Vyāghra Smṛti*. (5) There is a controversy between Dr. Kane and Dr. Apte V.M. on the point of *Vrata*. This is already referred[39] to by Dr. Kane and his rejoinder in the first part of the fifth Volume of the *History of Dharmaśāstra*. Dr. R.N. Dandekar high- handedly says that the interpretations suggested by both Kane and Apte are unacceptable[40] to him personally. As Dr. Dandekar has not clarified his stand-point with some Vedic evidence so far, his opinion need not be taken seriously.

Now we turn to a few cases of improvement on the part of Dr. Kane. As regards the expression *'Āmikṣā'* Dr. Kane's explanation in his notes on the *Harṣacaritam* p. 94 is based on Sanskrit dictionary. The same is the case with the explanation given by Ranganātha on the *Harṣacaritam*. It is MM. Dr. Ganganatha Jha who has given the correct explanation in his *Mīmāṁsā-Maṇḍana* p. 162. But it must be stated here that if one consults Dr. Kane's *History of Dharmaśāstra* Vol. II/II p. 1092 and particularly the foot-note No. 2448, one would be convinced that Dr. Kane has given more correct explanation here. This is a proof of improvement on the part of Dr. Kane particularly in comparison with the Note on the *Harṣacaritam* and the *History of Dharmaśāstra*. (2) One may cite one more case. Dr. Kane has correctly explained the word *'Upasangrahaṇam'* when it occurs in the *Harṣacaritam*. In his notes p. 57, he translates it as 'who made a respectful salutation.' Even Ranganātha, the commentator of the *Harṣacaritam* explains it. These two explanations, though satisfactory from the point of view of a general reader, will not satisfy the interested readers of Dharmaśāstra. For a proper explanation of this word, however, attention may be drawn to Dr. Kane's explanation in the *History of Dharmaśāstra* Vol. II/I pp. 334-225. This explanation again is a case of improvement in the writings of Dr. Kane. It appears that while writing the *History of Dharmaśāstra*, he has done complete justice to such words as have occurred in his notes on the *Harṣacaritam.* (3) In the collection of papers of Dr. Kane which I am going to present to the scholarly world in the book one will notice the tendency in Dr. Kane's writings that he has always made improvement over the matter presented previously and also added more matter to the previous articles. Here, in passing, it may be noted that Dr. Kane's note or a chapter in the third Volume of the *History of Dharmaśāstra*, particularly on *Kalivarjyam*, one will notice the addition of respectable amount of matter. Some of his papers will satisfy this requirement. This is a sure proof of his improvement and addition to the subject and when he went on reading and finalising the matter. The same may be said about Asahāya, the commentator of the *Gautama-Dharma-Sūtra*. Dr. Kane has added in his *History of Dharmaśāstra* Vol. I/I p. 548 that Asahāya probably wrote a commentary on the *Manu-Smṛti* also. This may be treated as a case of addition to his views on Asahāya.

It is always said that the study of the Dharmaśāstra cannot be said to be complete without the study of Pūrva-Mīmāṁsā. Dr. Kane has written a chapter on *'Mīmāṁsā and Dharmaśāstra'* in the fifth volume of the *History of Dharmaśāstra* pp. 1152 to 1351. Here he has explained the Mīmāṁsā doctrines, theories and clarified the matter with the help of Dharmaśāstra and Pūrva-Mīmāṁsā. This has influenced Dr. Moghe and others. One may clarify this point by stating that the contribution of the writers on Dharmaśāstra like Aparārka,[41] Vijñāneśvara,[42] Śūlapāṇi[43] and Mitramiśra,[44] the commentators of the *Yājñavalkya-Smṛti*, Kullūkabhaṭṭa,[45] the commentator of the *Manu- Smṛti*, Haradatta[46] and Maskari,[47] the commentators of the *Āpastaṁbha* and *Gautama Dharma Sūtras*, digest authors like Nīlakaṇṭha[48] and Śankarabhaṭṭa,[49] Devaṇṇabhaṭṭa,[50] Raghumaṇi,[51] Mādhavācārya, the commentator of the *Parāśara Smṛti.* (2) In addition to this, Dr. Moghe has also brought to light the contribution of some authors like Medhātithi for *Anuvāda*, Mitramiśra[52] for *samuccaya*. He has also guided a thesis[53] on *'Mīmāṁsā in Medhātithi'* for the Ph.D. Degree. (3) Besides, he has evaluated the contribution of Śaṅkarācārya,[54] and Sāyaṇācārya[55] for the domain of Pūrva-Mīmāṁsā. (4) Further, he has given a serious consideration to the important topics like Pūrva-Mīmāṁsā[56] and Astrological interpretation and Pūrva-Mīmāṁsā[57] and Paurāṇic interpretation (particularly the Dharmaśāstra material in the Purāṇas interpreted by the Dharmaśāstra authors from the Mīmāṁsā angle. (5) He has also brought to light some common aspects[58] of the

Paribhāṣās of Vyākaraṇa and the Mīmāṁsā rules of interpretation. (6) He has also made a proper comparison[59] between the two commentaries *Sāravivecanī* and *Prabhā* on the *Mīmāṁsānyāyaprakāśa* of Āpadeva. (7) He has also made the proper evaluation[60] of the contribution of MM. Dr. P.V. Kane to the domain of Pūrva- Mīmāṁsā, by presenting a special article in MM. Dr. P.V. Kane Commemoration Monograph published by the University of Bombay in the year 1974. (8) He has further advocated the evolutionary theory of the science of Pūrva- Mīmāṁsā, by writing papers on *Atideśa,*[61] *Punarvacana,*[62] *Vākyabheda*[63] and *Ūha.* (9) His two works *Mīmāṁsā discussions on Śrāddha-Sāgara of Kullūkabhaṭṭa* and Alaṁkāra śāstra are in progress and will see the light of the day very soon. (10) Dr. Moghe has also shown how the Mīmāṁsā principles of interpretation are utilised by the writers on classical Sanskrit works and the *Kāmandakīya*[64] *Nītisāra.* This small survey will reveal that there is a good progress in respect of the studies of Dharmaśāstra and Pūrva- Mīmāṁsā.

It will not be out of place, if only incidentally some important aspects of Dr. Kane's research work are high-lighted in the light of the papers which have no place in his volumes of *History of Dharmaśāstra*. In doing this, some times the purpose at the back of the mind of the present author is indicated for the future guidance of the workers on Indology. (1) In a paper on '*Dharma-Sūtra of Śaṅkha-Likhita*[65], Dr. Kane has restored the text of the two Dharmaśāstra authors, Śaṅkha and Likhita in the light of the works he has relied upon. It will be an opportunity to the workers of Indology to compare other published works on Dharmaśāstra and add to the passages which have no place in the collection of the passages by Dr. Kane. (2) In a paper on 'the *Arthaśāstra*[66] of Kauṭilya Dr. Kane has expressed his views on the authenticity of the text, its relation to the *Manu-Smṛti,* Kāmaśāstra, herbs and drugs etc. (3) In a paper on '*The Pārijāta*[67] *and the Madana-Pārijāta*', Dr. Kane has discussed and concluded that the identity of the two works is not possible even chronologically and the two works are totally different from each other. Here the aspects of the identity and chronology of the works play very important part. (4) In a paper '*Vedic Mantras*[68] *and Legends in the Purāṇas*', Dr. Kane has shown the relation between the Vedic Mantras and the *Brahma-Purāṇa*. Here he has made two classifications. He first quotes the places of the *mantras* which are actually quoted verbatim in the *Brahma-Purāṇa* and in the second category , he has shown how the stanzas in the *Brahma-Purāṇa,* contain the good paraphrase of the Vedic *mantras*. This also reveals his knowledge of the Vedic literature along with the Paurāṇic niceties. (5) In an article[69] on *'Naming a Child or a Person'* Dr. Kane has made elaborate discussion on the practices in the Gṛhya Sūtras particularly in comparison with the Vedic literature. Incidentally, he has also considered the evidences from the *Mahābhāṣya* of Patañjali and the voluminous commentary of Aparārka on the *Yājñavalkya-Smṛti*. In fact, the present paper is an addition to the matter presented in the *History of Dharmaśāstra* Vol. II/I pp. 238-254. Thus, this paper reveals the aspect of fill up the gap in one's won work by Dr. Kane. (6) In a paper *'The Predecessors of Vijñāneśvara*[70] Dr. Kane has considered how Vijñāneśvara has examined the views of his predecessors like Asahāya, Viśvarūpa, Bhāruchi, Śrīkara and Medhātithi.

Here he has explored the vast Dharmaśāstra literature and noted the similarities and differences of Vijñāneśvara with these authors. Though it is true, that some points from this paper are utilised by Dr. Kane for his *History of Dharma-Śāstra* Vol. I/I, yet the elaborateness may be regarded as the special feature of this paper that is included in this bunch of papers. (7) In a paper on *'The Dvaita-Nirṇaya'*[71] *of Śaṅkarabhaṭṭa*, Dr. Kane has considered the manuscript of this work in the Deccan College Collection, Pune. This manuscript was later on published by J.R. Gharpure. In the year 1918, Dr. Kane has shown the importance of this manuscript from the view point of Mīmāṁsā discussions, the Purāṇas quoted by him and the way in which the debatable problems are solved by Śaṅkarabhaṭṭa. He has also placed his unerring finger on the importance of the line *'Dauhitro Bhāgineyaśca śūdrasyā' pi ca dīyate*. It is thus handling the source of the manuscript for the Dharmaśāstra purpose. It must be noted here that in the *History of Dharma-Śāstra*, there is no chapter on *Dvaitanirṇaya*, but in some volumes, there are references to this work. Hence the importance of this paper can hardly be denied. (8) In a paper on *'The Tantravārtika*[72] *and the Dharmaśāstra literature* Dr. Kane has considered the passages from the Āpastaṁba, and *Gautama Dhama Sūtras* quoted in the *Tantravārtika* and shown that the *Manu-Smṛti* XI. 10 is not to be considered as spurious; it is in fact, a genuine portion of the *Manu-Smṛti*, since this stanza is quoted by Kumārila in his comments on the *Mīmāṁsāsūtras*. The importance of this paper lies in the fact that this has no proper place in the *History of Dharmaśāstra* Vol. V/II, but this is of the inter-disciplinary type. (9) Dr. Kane has discussed in a paper entitled *'Asahāya,*[73] *the commentator of the*

Gautama Dharma-Sūtra and the Nārada-Smṛti, the contribution of the commentator Asahāya, whose commentary is not now available to us. Here he has collected the information from the commentaries of the Smṛti works like the Manu and the Yājñavalkya and the Hāralatā of Aniruddha. Getting information of an author whose work is not available from other sources forms the important aspect of this paper. (10) Dr. Kane has discussed the actions forbidden in the Kali age particularly in his paper on '*Kalivarjya*.'[74] This paper is properly elaborated by Dr. Kane in his *History of Dharma-Śāstra* Vol. III. The importance of this paper lies here in presenting the verses (quoted here in the Appendix) to this paper and which have no place in the monumental work of Dr. Kane. The verses have the bearing on the aspect of the things prohibited in the Kali Age. Herein lies the importance of this paper. (11) In a paper '*The Meaning of Ācāryaḥ*',[75] Dr. Kane has refuted the view point of Prof. K.V. Rangaswami Aiyangar, when he held the view by the word 'Ācārya', Kauṭilya refers to his own teacher. Here Dr. Kane has .led evidences from the *Nirukta. Mahābhāṣya*, Aparārka etc. to contrdict the above view. Hence this article has the research aspect of refutation of the view of others. In addition to this, this paper is only casually mentioned in the *History of Dharmaśāstra* Vol. I/I p. 209. (12) In a paper '*Passages from the Rājamārtaṇḍa*[76] *on Tithis, Vratas and Utsavas*, Dr. Kane has collected stanzas from the three manuscripts and identified the stanzas from the vast Dharmaśāstra literature. (13) Dr. Kane has discussed in a paper '*Purāṇa-Dharma-*'[77] how the Vedic *mantras* and legends are utilised in the Paurāṇic literature. Here he has also shown the Paurāṇic concept of *Dharma* and Pauraṇic ideas of sacrifices and pilgrimages and bathing in sacred places and has himself filled up the gap of his own work when he dealt with the meaning and sources of *Dharma*. It is thus the important aspect of his research that is revealed here. (14) In a paper on '*King Bhoja*[78] *and His works on Dharmaśāstra and Astrology*', Dr. Kane points out the works of Bhoja such as *Bhīmaparākrama, Bhujabalanibandha, Rājamārtaṇḍa*. and *Vyavahāra-Samuccaya*, and has appreciated importance of the relation of Astrology to Dharmaśāstra. In this paper, he has further mentioned the places where the manuscripts of these works are there. (15) Dr. Kane has discussed in a paper '*The Kauṭilya*[79] *and the Matsyapurāṇa*' the resemblances between the two works and concluded that the author of the *Matsyapurāṇa* seems to have borrowed the ideas from the Kauṭilya *Arthaśāstra*, though the date of the *Matsyapurāṇa* is said to be uncertain. Here he has actually cited the passages from both the works to enlighten the readers. (16) In a paper on *'Utpala and the Arthaśāstra of Kauṭilya'*. Dr. Kane has cited some passages from the commentary of Utpala on the *Yoga- yātra* of Varāhamihira, particularly from the *Kauṭilya-Arthaśāstra.* basing his discussion on a manuscript in the Bhau Daji Collection of Sanskrit manuscripts. (17) *Mahābhārata citations in the Śābara-Bhāṣya'* is a paper Dr. Kane wrote to fill up a gap of the paper or a chapter of Dr. V.M. Apte and Dr. D.V. Garge. Dr. Kane states here that some of the *Sūtras* of Jaimini read like verses or *pādas*.

The writer of this note takes an oppertunity to mention only incidentally some of the interesting papers on Dharmaśāstra to quench the thirst of the interested readers of Dharma-Śāstra. (1) *The Doctrine of Prāyaścitta in Hindu Law and Jaina Doctrine of Karma* by Y. Kishnan, in A.B.O.R.I. Vol. LXIV-1983. pp. 109-117. (2) *The Doctrine of Karma and Śrāddha* in A.B.O.R.I. Vol. LXVI, 1987 pp. 97-115. (3) *Caṇḍcāvera and His Rājanīti-Ratnākara* by Dr. M.D. Paradkar, in the *Mysore Orientalist* Vol. XIV. pp. 83-87. (5) *Position of Widows in Early Medieval India in the Light of the Kathāsaritsāgara* by Aparna Chattopadhyaya in JOI, Baroda. Vol. XXIV. Nos. 3 & 4, 1975, pp. 292-402. (6) *Gotra and Exogamy* by K.C. Mishra in JOI, Baroda, Vol. XXIV Nos. 3 & 4, 1975, pp. 422 to 427. (7) *Saṁskāras-Their purpose and significance* by Dr. M.D. Paradkar, in *Mysore Orientalist* Vol. IV. No. 1 1971. pp. 8-14. (8) *Bṛhaspati on State Patronage to Free Booters*, by Raghavendra Vajpeyi, Kane Centenary Volume issued by Asiatic Society of Bombay, 1977-78, pp. 212-217. (9) *Adoption-Unmarried woman* by H.S. Ursekar, in *Bharatīya Vidyā*, Vol. XXXIX No. 1. 1979, pp. 55,68. (10) *Law in Ancient India*, by Prof. R.P. Kangle, in *Bhāratīya Vidyā*, Vol. L, 1990 Nos. 1-4. pp. 50-57. (11) *Prostitution in Ancient India* by Dr. Krishna Murari, in JGJKSV, Vol. XLI, 1985, pp. 57-65. (12) *Śunaḥśepa and Dattaka-Vidhāna* by S.G. Moghe, in JGJKSV, Vol. XXXV- 1979, pp. 85-96. (13) *Dāsa Varṇa in the Ṛgveda* by Ram Gopal, in JGJKSV, Vol. XXXIV, 1978, pp. 1-12. (14) *Glimpses of Ācāra and Vyavahāra in Early Indian Literary and Epigraphic Records* by D.C. Sircar pp. 3-14 of the *Studies in Dharmaśāstra*. (15) *Father Bouchet's letter on the Administration of Hindu law* by Ludo Rocher, pp. 15-48 of the above volume. (16) *A Sanskrit Jayapatra from 18th Century Mithila* by Richard W. Lariviere pp. 49-80 of the above volume. (17) *Renouncer and Renunciation in the Dharmaśāstra* by Patrick Olivelle, pp. 81-152 of the above volume. (18) *Legal and Symbolic Significance of the Menstrual Pollution of Rivers* by Richard Salomon, pp. 153-178. (19) *What Dharmaśāstra has to say about Dowry* by J.D.M. Derrett, pp. 179-193 of the above volume. (It may be noted here that this book is edited by Richard W. Lariviere.) (20) *The Origin of the Gotra System in the Ṛgveda* by V.G. Rahurkar, in A.B.O.R.I., Vol. LIII-1972, pp. 95-99. (21) *Mahābhārata and Dharmaśāstras* by M. Bhavanachari, in J.H. Dave Volume issue by *Bharatiya Vidya*, pp. 253-259. (22) *The Theory and Practice of Punishment as Recorded in Vardhamāna Upādhyāya's Daṇḍaviveka.* by Bhabatosh Bhattacharya, in the proceedings of the A.I.O.C., 26th Session, 1972, pp. 225-244. In passing, it may be noted that the conclusion of the above papers does not mean that other papers are not worth recording. The only important thing is that I have no approach to all the journals in the world, or through oversight, some article may have escaped my notice.

I would like to close this article by making a specific reference to some of the important books that are published during the last thirty years. (1) *Dharmaśāstra and Juridical literature* by J.D.M. Derrett, pp. 1-75 published by Otto Harrassowitz. Wisebaden. (2) *The Socio-legal Position of Women in the Smṛtis of Manu and Yājñavalkya* (A Ph. D. thesis deposited in the Poona University, 1971) and an article on the above topic in Homage to Dr. Mainkar, pp. 1-17. (3) *Oaths and Ordeals in Dharma-Śāstra* a published Ph.D. thesis of Dr. S.N. Pendse, and deposited in the M.S. University of Baroda. (4) *Vipramiśra's Śrāddha- Pradīpa* with *Raśmi* commentary by Dr. B.K. Swain. (5) The *Vyāghra Smṛti* edited by Dr. S.G. Moghe, published by Bhandarkar Oriental Institute, Pune, 1985. (6) *Studies in the Dharma-Śāstra* (A collection of 35 papers on Dharma-Śāstra and Kauṭilya Arthaśāstra) by S.G. Moghe, published by Ajanta Books International, Delhi, 1991. (7) *A Critical Edition of the Śrādha-Sāgara of Kullūkabhaṭṭa* by Dr. S.G. Moghe, published by D.K. Printworld (P.) Ltd. Delhi, 1993. (8) *Mensturation in Ancient India, by Dr. (Smt.) Sarala Srinivasan. (9) Slavery in Ancient India,* by Dr. Dev Raj, published by people's publication House, New Delhi, 1960. *(10) Studies in the Pūrva-Mīmāṁsā* (a collection of 22 papers) by S.G. Moghe, published by Ajanta Books International, Delhi, 1984. (11) *Studies in Applied Pūrva-Mīmāṁsā* (A collection of 22 papers) by S.G. Moghe will be very shortly published by Ajanta Books International, Delhi, 1995. (12) *Dāya-Vibhāga* by I.S.P Wate, published by Karnatak University. Dharwar, 1979. (13) *The Indian Society in the Mahābhārata* by

S.C. Bennerji. (14) *The Sacrament of Marriage in Hindu Society* by Miss. U.M. Apte. (15) *Mīmāṁsā, the Vākyaśāstra in Ancient India* (A Ph.D. thesis partly published) by Dr. G.V. Devasthali. (16) *Smṛti- Material in the Mahābhārata* by Dr. S.C. Bannerji, published at Calcutta.

By writing this very lengthy article, I feel that I have taken a survey of the Dharmaśāstra literature-articles, Books and Ph.D. thesis, indicated the progress in the subject, made suggestions for the future workers of Indology and thereby paid my respectful tribute to the sacred memory of that great scholar MM. Dr. Pandurang Vaman Kane, the like of him will not be seen for a long long time to come.

REFERENCES

1. A.B.O.R.I. Vols. VII and VIII.
2. The *Vyāghra Smṛti* published by B.O.R.I. Pune, 1985.
3. For the peculiar views of Ṛṣyaśṛṅga, *the Mysore Orientalist* Vol. XIV. pp. 66-67; Also see Dr. Moghe's *Studies in the Dharma-Śāstra*, pp. 67-68.
4. Prof. M.L. Wadekar, Devala-Smṛti. Ph.D thesis (two volumes) published by Bharatiya Kala Prakashan, Delhi, 1997.
5. P.V. Kane, History of Dharma-Śāstra Vol. I/II p. 1131 refers to this manuscript of 'Śvaśrū-snuṣā- Dharma-Saṁvāda as per Burnell's catalogue of Tanjore manuscripts p. 143a.
6. Miss Parvati S. Moholkar has written a thesis entitled 'A Critical edition of the Vivādacandra of Misaru-Miśra' particularly guided by Dr. Moghe. This thesis is deposited in the library of the University of Bombay, 1984.
7. Dr. S.G. Moghe, The Vyāghra-Smṛti 'Introduction pp. 18-21.
8. 'Ṛṣyaśṛṅga-Smṛti' restored, Mysore Orientalist, Vol. XIV p. 67.
9. Also see this paper published in Dr. Moghe's Studies in the Dharma-Śāstra, pp. 165-171.
10. A paper on 'A Fresh Interpretation of the Manu-Smṛti III. 162 published in the Bharatiya Vidya, Vol. XXXIX-1979, pp. 59-63.
11. Dr. Moghe's paper on 'Śunaḥśepa and Dattaka Vidhāna' published in the Journal of the Ganganatha Jha Kendriya Sanskrit Vidyapitha, Allahabad. Vol. XXXV, Parts 1-2. 1979, pp. 85-95.
12. Dr. Moghe, Studies in the Dharma-Śāstra, consult pp. 172- 177 for Abhinvagupta's novel interpretaton of the Gautama-Dharma- Sūtra IX. 35.
13. Dr. Moghe's paper on 'Kautilīya Arthaśāstra III. 5.28-A Reappraisal' in *Studies in the Dharma-Śāstra*, pp. 240-244. Also see this paper published in the Journal of the Oriental Institute, Baroda, Vol. XXXVI, Nos. 1-4, 1986-1987, pp. 97-101.
14. Also see the paper 'Significance of Ananyapūrvikā in the Yājñavalkya-Smṛti' published in the *Studies in the Dharma-Śāstra*, pp. 159-164.

15. For the significance of Nyāsa, see Dr. Moghe's '*A Peep at Indology*' pp. 35-42; also see 'Dharma-Śāstra concept of Nyāsa and Sanskrit Literature' published in the *Journal of Oriental* Research Institute, Tirupati, Vol. XXX-1987, pp. 87-94.
16. For the meanings of Bhrūṇa, see Dr. Moghe's paper 'Dharma-Śāstra Aspects of the Rāmāyaṇa' published in his book '*A Peep at Indology*, pp. 31-32.
17. 'Concept of Witness in the Mahābhārata and Dharma- Śāstra literature' published in a book '*A Peep at Indology*', pp. 19022. Also see Oriental Journal Venkateshvara University, Vols. XXXIII. XXXXIV, 1989-91, pp. 135-139.
18. A.B.O.R.I. Vol. LXIV of 1983, consult p. 263 for the peculiar views of Buddha. Also see this paper published in the '*Studies in the Dharma-Śāstra*' p. 56.
19. S.G. Moghe, The Vyāghra-Smṛti 'Introduction pp. 27-28 for the concept of 'Svayaṁpāka' in the context of Śrāddha.
20. For the concept of a widow, consult Dr. Moghe's *Studies in the Dharma-Śāstra*, pp. 183-190 and particularly p. 184 of the article 'Smṛtis. Smṛtikāras and Digest authors: Retrospect and Prospect'.
21. Hemādri's Darpaṇa p. 132.
22. Relation of the Gṛhya Sūtras to the Dharma-Śāstra literature' by Dr. S.G. Moghe in Tattvāloka, Vol. V. No. 1. April 1982, pp. 15-28. Also see 'Studies in the Dharma-Śāstra, pp. 1-12.
23. Relation of Kāmaśāstra to the Dharma-Śāstra by Dr. S.G. Moghe in Bhāratīya Vidyā, Vols. XLV, XLVI, XLVII for 1985-86-87, pp. 126-136; Also see this paper in 'Studies in the Dharma-Śāstra, pp. 13-26.
24. Relation of the Indian Medical Science (Āyurveda) to Dharma- Śāstra' by Dr. Moghe in Bhāratī-Śodha-Sāra-Saṁgraha, Vol. II, 1973, pp. 51-57. Also see this paper published in the 'Studies in the Dharma-Śāstra' pp. 27- 35.
25. Dharma-Śāstra and Sanskrit Lexicons by Dr. Moghe published in the book 'Studies in the Dharma-Śāstra, pp. 25-40.Dr. S.N. Deo 'Dharma-Śāstra thoughts in Classical Sanskrit literature (from Bhāsa to Śrī-Harṣa, the author of the Naiṣadhīyacaritam' a Ph.D. thesis in the library of the Marathwada University. This thesis written in the Marathi language is deposited in the year 1993.
27. Dr. Moghe's paper 'Vaidyanātha Dīkṣita' published in the Journal of the Asiatic Society of Bombay, Vols. 60-61, pp. 56- 61. Also see this paper published in 'Studies in Dharma- Śāstra', pp. 165-171.
28. A few smṛtis may be mentioned here. Hārita, Saṁvarta, Laugākṣi, Viśvāmitra, Marīci, Prajāpati, Pracetas, Paiṭhinasi, Dakṣa, Pitāmaha, Karṣṇājini, etc. It may be remarked here that Dr. Kane's treatment on these Smṛtis is meagre.
29. Kapila-Smṛti, Vāhūla-Smṛti, Lohita-Smṛti, Nārāyaṇa-Smṛti, Kaṇva-Smṛti, Dālbhya-Smṛti, Bhāradvāja Smṛti, etc. are printed in the volumes of the Smṛti-Sandharbha by Mansukharai Mor, from Calcutta. It is observed that though these smṛtis were published before the revision of the first volume of History of Dharma-Śāstra; otherwise he would have given a thorough treatment to these Smṛtis, in keeping with his other chapters or sections on the smṛtis. Hence a work on these smṛtis is a desideratum.
30. Dr. Moghe's paper on 'Nīlakaṇṭha's Vyavahāra- Mayūkha and Śvaśrū-snuṣā-

Dhana- Saṁvāda' was published in the *Journal of the Asiatic Society of Bombay, Vols. 52-53/ 1977-78 pp. 200-207 (This Volume is treated as MM. Dr. Kane Birth Centenary Volume).*

31. Dr. Moghe's paper on 'The Hindu Adoptions Act-Ancient, Medieval and Modern : A comparison' was published in the Journal of the Oriental Institute, Baroda, Vol. XL Nos. 3-4, March-June 1991. pp. 235-242; Also see this paper published in 'Studies in the Dharma-Śāstra', pp. 134-141.
32. This has a reference to 48 Bom. L.R. 196.
33. P.V. Kane, History of Dharma-Śāstra, Vol. III pp. 801-802.
34. Dr. Moghe's paper on 'Are women entitled to perform sacrifices?' is published in 'Studies in the Dharma-Śāstra, pp. 190- 194.
35. Dr. Moghe's paper on 'Dāna section of the Dharma- Śāstra (based on the Mahābhārata) published in 'Studies in the Dharma-Śāstra', pp. 196-197 for the rates of donation. Also see 'Prasanna-Pārijata' (Datta Maharaja Kavisvara Felicitation volume in Marathi), 1990, pp. 89-93.
36. Dr. Moghe's paper on 'A Fresh Interpretaton of the Manu-Smṛti III. 162' is published in the Bharatiya Vidya, Vol. XXXIX No. 1 pp. 59-63; Also see this paper published in 'Studies in the Dharma-Śāstra', pp. 41-46.
37. Dr. P.V. Kane's paper on 'Tilaka Mark' in the Ṛṣi- Kalpanyāsa, p. 289.
38. *Tilakena Vinā vipro puṇyastrī kunkumam vinā. dvau etau garhitau loke daive pitreye ca karmaṇi St.* 192 of the Vyāghra-Smṛti edited by Dr. S.G. Moghe, p. 69.
39. Dr. P.V. Kane, History of Dharma-Śāstra', Vol V. Part I pp. 1021 for the controversy between Dr. Kane and Prof. V.M. Apte on the point of Vrata.
40. Dr. R.N. Daddekar's paper on 'Professor P.V. Kane - A Tribute' published in MM. Dr. P.V. Kane Commemoration Monograph published by the University of Bombay. Here particularly p. 11 may be read with advantage for the above remark of the writer of this note.
41. S.G. Moghe, Aparārka as a Mīmāṁsaka, Indian Antiquary, Third Series, Vol. V. No. 2, April 1971, pp. 27-92. S.G. Moghe, Nyāyas in the Commentary of Aparārka on the Yājñavalkya-Smṛti-G.J.K.S.V., Allahabad, Vol. XXVI, Part-4, 1970- pp. 47-54.
42. S.G. Moghe, Vijñāneśvara and Pūrva- Mīmāmsā, Vishvesahvaranand Indological Journal, Vol. VII. Parts i-ii. 1969, pp. 89-94. Also see Dr. Moghe's paper published as Vijñāneśvara and Nīlakaṇṭha as the Interpreters of the Yājñavalkya-Smṛti, Oriental Journal. Tirupati, Vol. XII, Parts 1 & 2, 1969, pp. 19- 29.
43. S.G. Moghe, On Śūlapāṇi- The interpreter of the Yājñavalkya-Smṛti, Oriental Journal, Tirupati, Vol. XVII, Parts I and 2, pp. 113-121.
44. S.G. Moghe, 'A few Observations on Mitramiśra' - The Commentator of the Yājñavalkya, *Smṛti- Pratibhanam* (Dr. P.K. Narayana Pillai, Felicitation Volume, 1970 issued by Kerala Institute) pp. 45-56.
45. S.G. Moghe , 'The Position of Kullūkabhaṭṭa as a Mīmāṁsaka', Bharatiya Vidya, Vol. XXVIII., Nos-1-4, 1968, pp. 94-102. S.G. Moghe - 'Mīmāṁsa Passages in the commentary of Kullūka on the Manu-Smṛti'- Journal of the Oriental Institute and Manuscripts Library, Kerala, Vol. XVIII, Nos. 1 & 3, pp. 139-150.

46. S.G. Moghe, 'Haradatta as a Mīmāṁsaka' Journal of the Oriental Institute, Baroda, Vol. xx, No. 3. pp. 208-215.

47. S.G. Moghe, 'Haradatta and Maskari as the Interpreters of the Gautam- Dharma-Śāstra- G.J.K.S.V., Allahabad, Vol. XXXIII, Part 2, pp. 65-84, 1977.

48. S.G. Moghe, 'Nīlakaṇṭha as a Mīmāṁsaka' - *Umesh Mishra Commemoration Volume* by G.J.K.S.V., Vol. XXIV, parts 1-4, 1968, pp. 87-99. Also see Dr. Moghe's paper on 'A new light on Nīlakaṇṭha', *Indian Antiquary*, Third Series, Vol. V. No. 3, 1071, pp. 144-153.

49. S.G. Moghe, 'Nīlakaṇṭha's Indebetedness to Śaṅkarabhaṭṭa'- *Journal of the University of Bombay*, No. 80- 81, Vol. XLIV - XLV - October 1975-76, pp. 37-47.

50. S.G. Moghe, The use of the Mīmāṁsā maxims in the Smṛticandrikā of Devaṇṇabhaṭṭa'. (2) and (3) The use of Mīmāṁsā and popular maxims in the Smṛticandrikā of Devaṇṇabhaṭṭa'. All these are published in the Journal of the Oriental Research Institue and Manuscripts Library, University of Kerala, Vol. XVII, No. 4, Vol. XIX, part 2, and Vol. XV Part I.

51. S.G. Moghe, Dattaka-Chandrikā, published in Oriental Journal, Tirupati, Vol. XXI-XXII, 1978-79, pp. 61-68.

52. S.G. Moghe, Samuccaya- A Neglected Mīmāṁsā term by Vijñāneśvara, A.B.O.R.I. Vol. L.I, 1970, pp. 83-92.

53. A.R. Joshi, Mīmāṁsā in Medhātithi' - A Ph.D. thesis guided by Dr. S.G. Moghe, is deposited in the library of the University of Bombay, 1983.

54. S.G. Moghe, Śaṅkarācārya and Pūrva- Mīmāṁsā' - *Mysore Orientalist*, Vol. IV, No. 2, 1971, pp. 79-89. Also see his paper on 'Śaṅkarācārya's approach to Arthavāda'- published in *Journal of the Oriental Institute*. Tirupati, Vol. XXVII, parts 1-2, 1984, pp. 43-56.

55. S.G. Moghe, Sāyaṇācārya's Equipment of Pūrva- Mīmāṁsā' - *Journal of the Oriental Institute*, Baroda, Vol. 24, Nos. 3 & 4 1975, pp. 257-268.

56. S.G. Moghe, Pūrva-Mīmāṁsā and Paurāṇic Interpretation', Purāṇa Journal, Vol. XIX, No. 2, 1977, pp. 283- 291.

58. S.G. Moghe, Paribhāṣās of Vyākaraṇa and the Mīmāṁsā Rules of Interpretation - A Comparative Study, published in '*Ṛṣi-Kalpa-nyāsa - Rajeshvara Shastri Felicitation Volume*, 1970, pp. 90-100.

59. S.G. Moghe, The Comparative Study of the Commentaries Sāravivecinī and Prabhā on the Mīmāṁsā- nyāya-prakāśa of Āpadeva' - *Bharatiya Vidya*, Vol. XL. Nos. 203, 1980, pp. 95-100.

60. S.G. Moghe, MM. Dr. P.V. Kane's Contribution to the Domain of Pūrva-Mīmāṁsā' - in *MM. Dr. P.V. Kane Commemoration Monograph* (published by the University of Bombay, 1974) pp. 83-99.

61. S.G. Moghe, The Evolution of the Mīmāṁsā technical term Atideśa', A.B.O.R.I. (Diamond Jobilee Volume 1977-78) pp. 777-784.

62. S.G. Moghe, Motivations of Punarvacana', *Journal of the Asiatic Society of Bombay*, Vols. 49,50,51/1974-75,76, pp. 128-135.

63. S.G. Moghe, Some Evolutionary Aspects of Vākyabheda J.G.J.K.S.V., Vol. 37, Parts 1-4, 1983 (*Prof. Baladeva Upadhyaya Felicitation Volume*), pp. 169-187.

64. S.G. Moghe, 'Mīmāṁsā Principles as envisaged by Śaṅkarācārya in Jayamaṅgalā on the Kāmandakīya Nītisāra' J.G.J.K.S.V. Allahabad, Vol. XLII, pp. 121-130.
65. P.V. Kane, Śaṅkhalikhita Dharma-Sūtra- A.B.O.R.I. Vols. VII and VIII.
66. P.V. Kane, Arthaśāstra of Kauṭilya - A.B.O.R.I., Vol. VII, 1926, pp. 101-128.
67. P.V. Kane, Pārijāta and Madanapārijāta- Procedings of the A.J.O.C.XII0 II pp. 267-272, 1943-44.
68. P.V. Kane, Vedic Mantras and legends in the Purāṇas, Raja Commemoration Volume, pp. 5-14, Madras, 1946.
69. P.V. Kane, Naming a child or a person, Indian Historical quarterly, XIV, 1938, pp. 224-244.
70. P.V. Kane, Prodecessors of Vijñāneśvara-JBBRAS (new series), I, 1925, pp. 193-224.
71. P.V. Kane, Dvaitanirṇaya - A.B.O.R.I. Vol. III, 1921, pp. 67- 72.
72. P.V. Kane, Tantravārtika and the Dharma-Śāstra literature, JBBRAS (new series) I, 1925.
73. P.V. Kane, Asahāya, the commentator of the Gautama of the Gautama Dharma Sūtra and the Dharma-Smṛti, in JBORC VIII- II, 1922, pp. 120-124.
74. P.V. Kane, Kalivarjaya', in JBBRAS (New Series), XII, 1936, pp. 1-18.
75. P.V. Kane, 'Meaning of the Ācāryaḥ'; A.B.O.R.I., XXIII, 1942, pp. 206-214.
76. P.V. Kane, 'Passages from the Rājamārtaṇḍa on Tithis, Vratas and Utsavas,' A.B.O.R.I., XXXVI, 1956, pp. 306- 339.
77. P.V. Kane, 'Purāṇa-Dharma', *Gode Commemoration Volume*, 1960, pp. 70-82.
78. P.V. Kane, 'King Bhoja and His works on Dharmaśāstra and Astrology', JOR, XXIII, 1953-54, pp. 94-127.
79. P.V Kane, Kauṭīlya and Matsya Purāṇa' *Law Commemoration Volume*, Poona, 1946, pp. 13-15.
80. P.V. Kane, Utpala and the Arthaśāstra of Kauṭilya, A.B.O.R.I., XXVIII, 1948, pp. 136-137.
81. P.V. Kane, Mahābhārata Citations in the Śābara- Bhāṣya', A.B.O.R.I., XXVIII, 1948, pp. 135-136.

6

RESEARCH IN INDOLOGY : SCOPE AND MODERN TREND WITH SPECIFIC REFERENCE TO THE ACADEMIC WORLD OF UNIVERSITIES OF GUJARAT

Vasant Parikh

The *Encyclopedia Britanica* offers following explanation about research. Research is the act of searching into a matter closely and careful inquiry directed to the discovery of truth, and in particular the trained scientific investigation of the principles and facts of any subject based on original and first hand study of authorities or experiment. Investigations of every kind which have based on original source of knowledge may be styled research and it may be said that without research no authorative works have been written.... no theories of any value propound.

After giving this general definition of research on a wider perspective the *Encyclopaedia* also refers to its some what limited and specific meaning saying, further that the term is particularly used at a post-graduated study at a university where a scholar devotes his time to the investigation at first hand of some specific subject.

We are interested here in this second aspect. For though independent research work in many a field is not less than the area covered by the university and allied institutions. It is more eloquent as the most of the published articles and books of this kind are the outcome of some research project that is aided, published or even patronised by U.G.C. or University or some academic institution. Here also publications are the doctoral theses.

Thus it is evident that the university students and scholars play a prominent role in this field at present especially in science, philosophy, linguistics and literature. From 19th century onwards Indology has been one of the most interested subjects for research. It took momentum after the foundation of Asiatic Society. Some areas in the culture and civilisation of India almost attracted scholars for their exploration. Western and Indian scholars alike plunged into the serious study of the history, archaeology, science, religion, philosophy, linguistics and literature of ancient India. Consequently a number of valuable volumes throwing light on new avenues and vistas of this ancient bank of knowledge were published. This new trend began to be recognised, accepted and pursued in the universities also. More and more scholars and post graduate students came forward with a spirit of dedication and enriched the Indological research by their important contribution. Dr. A.B. Dhurva, M.N. Trivedi, Durgaram Sastri, Pt. Shukalalji, Pt. Dalsukhabhai Malvania and Sandesara brothers are some of the great scholars of Indology. Revered Jaina Munis like Jinavijayaji and Punyavijayaji have done excellent job of collecting, preserving and also cataloguing a vast mass of manuscripts on Indology written in various scripts including Devanāgarī scripts with the result that manuscriptology was also considered a very essential branch of research in Indology in India.

In the light of this base and some what sketchy outline of research in Indology now let me appraise the study of this particular field in the Universities of Gujarat at present.

Research is pursued in different branches such as ;

Archaeological excavation

Arts like sculpture, music and paintings

Restructuring and revaluating the history of India in the light of fresh and authentic material

Different cultural, social and religious traditions

Philosophy

Linguistics and

Literature etc.

A casual survey of the post-graduate departments of Arts shows at a first glance that the students take up for their M. Phill, M. Lit, or Ph.D.

awards a specific subject as presented in the scriptures or literary works written mostly in Sanskrit and some times Prakrit also. Here also their target is limited in following aspects.

A critical study of some important topic of Vedic literature or epic. Critical study of a particular work or of an author. Study of some problems in various Śāstras like rhetoric, grammar and schools of philosophy etc. Comparative study of different systems or schools or literary works. Collecting and critically editing unpublished works preserved in manuscripts.

It is generally seen that a lot of critical studies is favoured most while the editing of manuscripts is prefered less. It will be good in the best interest of Indological studies if learned guides of Ph.D and M. Phil. encourage the students to undertake projects of collecting and brining out critical editions of some manuscripts on different subjects. Though we have got some valuable, critical or comparative studies, a number of such studies have disppointed us also. For we find in most of the thesis a mere compilation rather than a critical study. Originality and truth finding form the necleus of the research. Unfortunetely in most of the research works sometimes we find that what is claimed as original is not collaborated by truth and what is acclaimed as truth is not original. A basic knowledge of the fundamental norms of methodology is a pre-requisite of research.

Our research students should be taught these norms before they tread the path of research. Here are given some common rules to be followed for ready references.

— The scientific technique of observation or reading all the available literature, data-collection, elimination, forming of hypothesis, verification and deduction must be strictly observed.

— The sources of references must be clearly given in the foot-notes.

— Proper discrimination should be made in giving quotations. Quotations are either for the support or for refutation so the temptation of over flooding our work with quotations must be strictly controlled.

— Translation of any quotation from another language must be given.

— In absence of any solid and varifiable proofs, no theory or principle should be presented as final. It will be appropriate to present it in a form of suggestion that is open for further deliberations.

— Supplimentary material may be given in appendices and

— Bibliography must be given in proper order.

All these are common ingredients of research. Our future scholars are sure to enrich this vast and facinating field of research by their deligious study and spirit of learning.

7

RELEVANCE AND DIRECTION OF VEDIC STUDIES IN MODERN INDIA

Madhusudan Mishra

Preliminary

The term 'relevance' is, indeed, so vast in its semantic sphere that it includes and involves a number of aspects in it. Keeping the scope and wideness of the present topic in mind and problems involved therein, I prefer to be very much selective, specific and succint. Since the topic I have chosen includes two major items in it I shall divide my discussion into two different sections - Relevance of Vedic Studies in modern India, and Directions of Vedic Studies in modern India. In the first part, I shall present some aspects of Vedic literature which should be pursued vigorously through different types of studies. Keeping in mind the modern trend of thought and time these aspects are very much relevant at present. In the second, I shall make some difinite suggestions regarding the researches to be undertaken. This will include the works to be done and also the new approaches to be made so that new vistas of Vedic studies can be made upon.

1. Relevance of Vedic Studies

Time and space are the key factors which should be considered carefully while determining the relevance of any particular literature. Any change in time and space does necessarily initiate a change in the relevance of a particular literature. Thus keeping this in view, one has to determine the multi-faceted relevance of Vedic studies in modern India.

Of the main reasons as to why Vedic thought and civilization are still relevant and rich fields of facinating study lies in their unique structure, remarkable history and rare spirit of accomodating modern thought in it.

The history and culture of India deeply rooted in the Vedic literature, is of universal appeal and interest because of the light they throw upon the annals of human race. As one of the most ancient written records of human civilization, the Vedas are more relevant today than what they were during the times of their composition and compilation. This literature is truly an encyclopedia. The religious, socio-cultural, anthropological, magical, munial, medicinal, mythological, philosophical and physiological history of India, nay, of Asian civilization. The unorthodox spirit of Vedic religion is the true representation of Indian ethos.

The relevance of Vedic literature may be grouped under two major divisions. 1. Non-materialistic relevance and materialistic relevance.

Non-materialistic Relevance

Of utmost importance is our religious problem in India at present. The age-old secular fabric of India is facing an acid test today. It is becoming more grave and acute when an atmosphere of uncertainty, thoughtlessness and crisis is added to it. One is not absolutely sure as to on what platform he himself stands, what he should adhere to and what to abandon, who is he and what he stands for. The chaotic scenario prevailing at present stands testimony to that problem. It could be termed as an area of crisis and collision which is threatening the very foundation of our national edifice. This transition, if not handled properly, may lead to a cultural disaster. Thus there is an urgent need to mobilise our national ethos. And for that, the necessity of a truly secular religion is badly felt. To achieve this, Vedic studies are of high relevance at present.

Vedic religion has undergone a number of ordeals. In the long course of its evolution, it has adopted and accomodated various changes that have occured from time to time, without changing our basic structure. And for this aspect of its attitude it has efficiently served and would continue to serve as the perennial source of inspiration in modern India.

Vedic religion is a religion of humanity and humanism. It is not restricted to any particular creed as such. It has developed without a so-called religious scripture or book, since the Vedas could hardly be designated as the book of revelation in respect of that religion. No single person or prophet can claim to be the founder of this religion. It is free from the clutches of any charitable organisation or Church. No institutional rigidity controls it. It is a movement, not a stagnant eutopia; a process, not a result; a growing tradition, not a fixed revelation. Thus it has the inherent capacity to adjust itself with a truly modern culture. Humility is the manrow of its flow, not religious fundamentalism. It is a system of systems. Hence it embraces the whole humanity. From all these grounds, Vedic religion alone can tackle the crisis and confrontation resulting out of the classes between religion and religion, religion and modernity, obscurantism and adjustiveness. Vedism as a religion is a way of our life and not certainly a dogmatic code. This, as the true representative of Indian culture and civilization, will withstand all challenges, and boldly face them with its highly strong inherent power. Thus attempts should be made to highlight the secular character of Vedic religion which can bind the people of India in one thread.

Linguistic Relevance

Highly relevant are the Vedas from the linguistic point of view. As one of the oldest available literary records of the world, it serves as a basis for linguistic analysis. Comparative philology starts its journey from Vedic literature. Modern phonetics has its roots in the ancient *Śikṣā* treatises. Thus any linguistic analysis in India, nay, of Euro-Asia, will have to start from the Vedas. It reveals and will continue to reveal a number of data on the Asian as well as European continents. While justice has been given to classical Sanskrit by making an indepth and threadbare study of it. Vedic Sanskrit, on the other hand, has been highly neglected. As the oldest Indian, and at the same time, the oldest Indo-European literary monument, a complete and coherent study of Vedic linguistics must be given top priority in our agenda of research.

Cultural Relevance

The importance of Vedic studies from the point of view of the cultural history of India is of course, indisputable. Without the Vedic literature the history of India will not only remain wanting in nature but also certainly become distarted. The elaborate Vedic ritual system is a mine of information on subjects of high importance. Social-Anthropology has much to derive from it. There is hardly any doubt that the Vedic sacrifices had some kind of magic for their basis. Magic had indeed, been a very definite ring in that poor ladder up which our race still tries to climb in its efforts to ascertain the unknowable. A critical study of the Vedic ritual, particularly of the magic element in it, would, therefore, prove to be a very significant from larger anthropological point of view.

Philosophical and Mythological Relevance

The Vedas have played a significant role in creating a very strong and suitable background for the evolution of Upaniṣadic as well as Buddhist, Jaina and other philosophical systems. Thus comparative study of philosophy has to be initiated from Vedic Studies. Similarly comparative mythology is inaugurated with the study of Vedic mythology. With a view to ascertaining the genesis, growth, points of similarities and dissimilarties existing among different mythologies of the world and getting a complete and clear picture of the same, the study of Vedic mythology is to be pursued vigorously. Moreover, a number of religions viz. Buddhism will remain ever incomprehensible to them who do not know the Veda. It is the foundation on which other systems of thought are born and brought up. So from the point of view of comparative religion and mythology, the study of the Vedas is of profound importance and relevance.

Spiritual Relevance

The spiritual relevance of Vedic studies has always been quite prominent. The unabated flow of crisis and insecurity of the present time, the problems confronting India which have almost jeoparadised our progress even existence could not be adequately tackled on a more materialistic plane. The spiritual consciousness of the people needs to be awakened for that purpose. A truly spiritual treatise like the Veda would prove difinite step towards achieving that goal.

Literary Relevance

Lastly, the relevance of the Vedas from the literary point of view cannot be at all undermined. The study of comparative literature has to begin from this point. The genesis and growth at a number of literatures viz. poetry, prose, lyric, drama etc., have to be studied and analysed through and by this literary masterpiece. This historical approach will help enable us in knowing the mind and art of the people of one of the most ancient civilization of the world.

In addition to this, the *Sāmaveda*, beginner of Indian music still remains relevant to us. The beginning and gradual development of Indian magic can be brought to lime light by a deeper study of the Vedic literature. It is a maginificent inheritance and as long as this endures and influences the life and spirit of our soil and sons so long as the basic genius of India shall continue.

Materialistic Relevance

As regards this aspect of Vedic studies, the rapid advancement of modern science requires us to throw a little light on this. In this connection I would draw the attention of the scholars to the proceedings of the International Sanskrit Conference (Vol. III, Part I, Ed. by V. Raghavan, 1980) held on 1972 at New Delhi. This book is a mine of information exhaustively dealing with the vast content of positive sciences found in Vedic literature. However, I must be honest and candid to admit that the degree and state of modern sciences can hardly be seen therein. For, it is totally ridiculous to expect the present momentum of modern sciences in the treaties written millenia before today. Intensity and integration of scientific lore depend upon contemporary necessities and compulsions. Thus whatever science is available in the Vedic treatises should be regarded as the initial stage of science in general. They should be seen through an ancient eye. Any claim that the Vedas contain modern sciences in their present form must be outrightly rejected. According to me, if any branch of Vedic science deserves to be studied even today that is Vedic mathematics and Vedic Medicine.

1. It has been often claimed by scholars that Vedic Mathematics is more precise, easy and scientific than modern mathematical procedures involving many intricacies and elaborations. Bharati Krishna has exhibited the working of the sixteen sample mathematical formulae from the Vedas in his book *"Vedic Mathematics"*. It is illustrative of a host of others. He firmly puts forth his views that Vedic Mathematics, includes Trigonometry, Conics, Calculus, Algebra and Geometry etc., which extends to almost all branches of Mathematics. A solution to the so called Pithagoras theorem was given in the *Śulbasūtras* centuries before him. Thus, Vedic Mathematics would prove to be a sophisticated aid even today if it is studied with earnestness and in a scientific manner.

2. Vedic Medicines, particularly the ones described in the *Atharvaveda*, needs a serious approach. Placing of pounded banyan shoot in the nostrils of a wife during the *puṁsavana* ceremony is of immense importance. Secondly, when the wife is conducted to her husband's house, seated on the hide of a red bull, upon her lap is placed the son of a woman who had only borne living male children, it also refers to some important device. It is claimed that such acts refer to ancient Indian way of sex-determination. Atharvaṇic water therapy (AV. 6.24; 6.57) needs a cautious investigation. Use of various leaves for different diseases would also throw some light. So far as India is concerned, Vedic medicine may help the poorest of the poor, if studied properly. The detail description of human embryo given in the *Garbhopaniṣad* (śloka-2) needs a scientific investigation.

Directions of Vedic Studies in Modern India

To be absolutely candid, Indian scholarship, in comparison to its Western counterpart, has not been so successful in giving innovative directions to Vedic studies. Among a handful of epoch making directions that emanated from a few scholars of accumen the *Vedic Bibliography* of R.N. Dandekar, his theory of Vedic evolutionary mythology, Vaidika *Padānukramakośa* of Vishva Bandhu, *Śrautakosa* of C.G. Kashikar, Paṇḍit Satevalekar's edition of various Vedic texts deserve mention. Besides this, definite directions are seen in the works of Raghu Vir, Suryakanta, Durga Mohan Bhattacharya, Baladeva Upadhyaya, B.R. Sarma etc. But looking at the vastness of the field and extent of desiderata our overall situation does not appear to be encouraging. We still look towards the West for directions. Thus I wish to present a few suggestions in this regard.

1. Till now we have not been able to bring out critical editions of all the available Vedic texts. Besides a truly critically edited text of the *Ṛgveda*, by Vaidika Samsodhana Mandala, Poona along with Sāyaṇa's commentary, no other Saṁhitā in its entirety, with a commentary or two has been critically edited so far. However, it is indeed heartening to see that the critical edition of the Taittirīya saṁhitā with the commentaries of Sāyaṇa and Bhaṭṭa Bhāskara, edited by T.N. Dharmadhikari (Vidika Samsodhana Mandala, Poona,) has been completed upto the fifth *kāṇḍa*. Hopefully the remaining portions will be published soon. Another important recension of the Black

Yajurveda, namely the Maitrāyaṇi Saṁhitā is yet to get due attention. T.T. Dharmadhikari has been pursuing the work of its critical edition and we hope it will come out without further delay. The first fscicule being a specimen of his proposed critical edition has been published in *Kashikar Festschrift*.

2. *Vedic texts : a revision* (M.L.B.----). The Kaṇva saṁhitā, along with the commentaries of Sāysṇa, Ānandabodha and Anantācarya, critically edited by B.R. Sharma is now being published by the Vaidika Samsodhana Mandala, Poona. The first twenty *Adhyāyas* have been already published and the rest is under print. The critical edition of the Atharvaṇic Paippalāda Saṁhitā based on the Orissan manuscripts has been mercilessly held in since long after the sad demise of its editor Prof. D.M. Bhattacharya. It is learnt that Prof. Deepak Bhattacharya (Viswa Bharati, Santiniketan) and Miss Minati Pattanaik (Rourkela, Orissa) have been pursuing the editing work independently. However, a complete translation of this work in English is a work which is yet to be thought of. Since it involves great experience, care and caution, attempts should be made by established research institutions or a group of expert researchers to edit the complete text and translate the entire text into English. Thus our aim and energy should first be directed towards the critical editions of the saṁhitā texts along with commentaries thereon.

No edition is complete without a translation. In this regard I draw the attention of the scholars towards the translation of the Maitrāyaṇi Saṁhitā, preferably in English. In addition to this, translation of various Vedic texts available in German, French and other languages should be translated into English as it would wider the scope and help enable the non-German and non-French knowing scholars in getting an access to those books.

So far as the *Brāhmaṇas* are concerned, the *Kāṇva Satapatha Brāhmaṇa* is yet to come out in its entirety. The editing work of this text done by C.R. Swaminathan is complete now but is awaiting publication. Besides this the text of the *Brāhmaṇas* which are already published need a thorough revision in the light of the manuscripts discovered recently. For a comprehensive study of texts from various angles, translations of *Brāhmaṇa* texts in a foreign language preferably in English should be done. Of utmost priority is the translations of *Tittirīya Brāhmaṇa* and the *Gopatha Brāhmaṇa*.

Thirdly, most of the ritual sūtras need further revision in the light of the recent discoveries. C.G. Kashikar has done yeoman service by editing and translating the Bharadvāja *Śrautasūtra* and editing the Barāha *Srautasūtra*. However, the Varāha *Pariśiṣṭa* must be edited without further delay. Translation of the Baudhāyana *Srautasūtra* has been neglected till today. A number of commentaries on the Srautasūtras and independent *Srautaprayogas* should be brought out. Another important field of research which has not yet arrested our attention is the compilation of a *gruhyakośa* on the line of the *Srautakośa*.

This would help in a long way in determining the gradual development of the domestic rites in their historical perspective. Moreover this would also enable us to detect their deviation from the original practice, inclusion of non-Vedic subjects in their fold and the circumstances leading to such changes. Independent treatises focussing their attention on the various offerings given in Vedic ritual, significance of relevant myths in these rites, a comparative study of parallel performances if any, in any other religions would increase our insight regarding the Vedic sacrificial system at large. It will render rare help to reconstitute the socio-anthropological history of India.

The need for a complete dictionary carring all the Vedic words, showing their probable origins and relations with other Indo-European cognets is badly felt. A good number of new texts have come to light after the compilation of the *Vedic Dictionary* by Suryakanta. That book needs a through revision which should be carried out without delay.

A separate comprehensive Dictionary on Vedic rituals and ritualistic termonologies, impliments and utensils with various textul details and diagrams or photographs is a long felt need. Chitrabhanu Sen's work in this field is only a preliminary one and the one by T.N. Dharmadhikari (entitled *Yajñāyudhāni*) is too short a book to give a detailed idea about a topic of much magnitude.

A new Vedic concordance covering the texts not covered by M. Bloomfield should be prepared. It is indeed a happy news that the Tilak

Maharastra Vidyapeetha, Poona has undertaken this gignatic work under the able editorship of C.G. Kashikar.

Apart from the textul works, our study should also concentrate on the following vital issues involving Vedic researches. A comprehensive study of the three important aspects of Vedic literature namely, magic, music and medicine is highly needed. Unearthening the basis and structure of later Hindu religion, belief and customs in the Vedas would prove to be a nice field of study. The usefulness of the Vedic *mantras* not employed in any kind of item must be determined. Does it have any relation to any kind of worship? The criteria for choosing a particular *mantra* for a particular ritual perfermance should be discovered, the influence of Vedic literature on later Tantric and other allied cults has not been studied vigorously. Above all, an interdisciplinary approach towards Vedic studies would prove very much interesting which in turn will help us in restructuring the history of India.

While doing all this, no preconceived idea or notion should prevail over a scholar. No suggestion should be taken as final without being thoroughly examined. It does not matter from what a great authority it comes. For, sometimes, even the starting points are doubtful and conclusions are only possibilities.

A faithful study of Vedic culture and civilization requires familiarity with non-modern mentality with the then religious convictions and with the tradition of that society. Interpretation of every problem should be based on one's own reasoning and not on repeated or widespread popular conviction. Finally, our directions should have an orientation of modern philosophical and philological methods and knowledge of the history and culture of India. Foremost of all this is that every research should try to exhaust all this relevant facts on a given problem which, in turn results in giving a complete collection of all relevant materials on that problem. Above all, adequate steps should be taken to popularise the Vedic lore among the common mass which would help in creating an awareness among them regarding our rich ancient treasure.

BIBLIOGRAPHY

1. Dandekar, R.N. Some Aspects of the History of Hinduism, University of Poona, Poona (1967).

2. Filliozat, J. : The Classified Doctrine of Indian Medicine (Tr.) D.R. Channa, Delhi (1964).
3. Gonda, : *"Veda"*, New Horizors of Research In Indology, (Ed.) V.N. Jha, University of Poona, Poona (1989).
4. Kashikar, C.G. : The Srauta Ritual and the Vajapeya sacrifice, Poona (1955).
5. Thite, G.U.: Medicine: Its magic-Religious Aspects concerning to the Vedic and later Vedic literature, Poona (1982).

8

SOURCE MATERIAL IN SANSKRIT FOR INDOLOGICAL RESEARCH

B.K. Swain

Indological Research, basically started with the study of Sanskrit. Because, the original texts on the various branches of this vast field have been written in this language. Many older languages in general and Pali and Prākrit in particular have been the sister languages which have played no less role for all such studies. For the first time, the foreigners started systematic research on it in the modern sense of the term. The moment they could realise the treasures of Indology and its intrinsic value as enshrined in Sanskrit texts they started its analytical and comprehensive studies. Later on Indian scholars followed it and shouldered an ardous task of exploring its real essence entirely unknown so far. At the outset they followed the path of foreign scholars and in course of time, it is seen that, scholars where bound in someway or other had to rely mainly on the translation-work of those great foreign researchers, as a result of which original texts were relegated to the background. That is why research is, now a days, being carried on only on the basis of the secondary sources, sometimes amounting to both misinterpretation and misrepresentation of the reality. It is, no doubt, very dangerous. It is known after varification that many mistakes have been incorporated in the first hand works which create undesirable confusion on very serious points, sometimes amounting to serious controversies.

In this juncture, it is the main work of present day researchers in the line to go through the original texts and to re-interprete those by the sound techniques of modern methodology which would help to set a standard and which will, no doubt, pave the way for true understanding that the foreign scholars have actually intended to put forth. It can, definitely, be said that knowledge of Sanskrit coupled with adequate grasp over modern research methodology are badly essential. It is not to be construed that any competitive intellectual compilation under any methodology can be treated as a sound research work. Any standard work of Indology can claim the status of scientific research in this discipline only when it is based on the accepted seven-staired effort :

(i) Study of original text,
(ii) Review of works previously done,
(iii) Ascertainment of problems to be dealt with,
(iv) Selection of source, placement of arguments, determination of original finding,
(v) Supporting views of the parenthesis,
(vi) Refutation of cross-points and
(vii) Suggestion to the reader for undertaking similar project.

upakramopasaṁhārāvabhyāso'pūrvatā phalam/
arthavādopapattī ca liṅgaṁ tātparyanirṇaye//

Young scholars, interested to undertake different hypotheses to substantiate, are required to do so under the indigenous methodology and the modern way of presentation and sound knowledge of Sanskrit who would go a long way in bringing to the reader the real essence of what actually the Indian saints, seers and *Śāstrakāras* have left for the posterior generation.

9

NEEDS AND PROBLEMS OF INDOLOGICAL RESEARCH

Gopinatha Mohapatra

The term Indology is a foreign innovation in the study of Sanskrit and culture of India which has been brought to light since more than a century in a brighter form. The foreign scholars called India instead of Bhārata as they were calling the river Sindhu as Indus. As per their opinion the Indus Valley is later called on to be India which was not confined gradually within the Indus Valley but so extensively from the Himālayas to Kanyā Kumārī. The people here were called Hindus which has got its root from the river Sindhu. Thus India and the Hindus, both these terms have been misnomers for Bhārata and Aryans respectively. However, being originated from the western minds, both these terms, India and the Hindus have been popular all over the world and we, the Indians also gladly use these terms without hesitation.

The foreign scholars when wanted to study the Indian classical languages and culture, they named it as Indology. The word gradually became popular all over the world and now we the Indians use that term within India itself. It is because, the line in which the foreign scholars worked on the Indological studies and researches, became more interesting, useful, enlightening and scientific disciplined; so that everywhere it is admired and followed by the scholars at large.

There was a time when Sanskrit Kāvyas, the Vedas, Grammar, Smṛtis etc., were memorised by the scholars and this was a painful task, Those people used to complete their life time in getting by heart only two or three books and were remaining in darkness so far as other disciplines are concerned. However, the need of Sanskrit study and the study of Indology was felt in the Western countries, when they wanted to develop the studies under various disciplines in which they were working upon. The fields of linguistics, religion, comparative grammar, comparative philosophy, history, geography, culture, science, social science, Art and architecture, music and dance, archaeological studies, medicine and alchemy, rituals, comparative view on Paṇḍita tradition and western Epistemes in Indology, Environmental studies and so on ultimately attracted the scholars at large to take up the study of Indology in the various countries of the world. As a result, the office of the International Association of Sanskrit Studies was framed in the world level where the professors, and scholars of various countries on Indology are the members. This organisation holds world Sanskrit Conferences in three years intervals in different parts of the world. The exchange of thoughts in Indology has become so essential and useful in the present age that a pannel is working on the utility of Sanskrit through the modern device computer. The graphs, diagrams, tables etc., have been employed in the study of Indology.

Under these circumstances, the scholars of India should not sit idle in not opening the mind for the study of modern Indology as it is called and importance should be given on the studies of inter-disciplinary researches. This would help India to progress ahead alongwith the scholars of Indology working in different countries of the world. It is advisable therefore to have a touch for research in this line of interdisplinary nature with the universities and institutions working abroad like Oxford, Harvard, Pennsylvania, Torine University, University of Stockholm, University of Tokyo, London University, University of Paris, University of Borlin, Tubngen University, University of Vienna, University of British Columbia, Chicago University, La Trobe University, University of Helsinki and so on. The Indian Universities working at Delhi, Poona, Benaras, Santiniketan, Calcutta, Baroda, Sagar, Jabalpur, Trivendrum, Madras etc., are some of the important centres in the fields of general research. However, with a view to the modern trend of mind some other professors have arranged Seminars on Sanskrit through computer, studies on Purāṇas which would be the milestones in the progress of modern trend of research in Sanskrit. Otherwise, for how many years again the Indian Sanskrit scholars would play the drums with the traditional theories of Rasa, Dhvani, Rīti, Alaṅkara, Pāṇini Sūtras, Advaitavāda, Dvaitavāda, etc., closing the eyes towards the interdisciplinary side of research which is helpful and benificial for all other disciplines of the knowledge at large. It was my good privilege that I had to chair twice in World Sanskrit Conferences in Vienna and Melbourne where I found the scholars belonging to different faculties other than Sanskrit and presented papers on Sanskrit studies. Even in Melbourne, it was found in the world Sanskrit Conference, that some of the Professors of Science subjects like Chemestry etc. took part with active interest in Sanskrit. In this centext it is however remarkable to note as to how many Professors of other subjects and the high officers of India are serious to read *Śrīmad Bhagavad Gītā, the Rāmāyaṇa* and *Mahābhārata* for which we are so proud of. Under these prevailing circumstances, however, a lot of Indian scholars have worked in interdisciplinary researches with a modern outlook and therefore Prof. R.N. Dandekar, Prof. R.K. Sharma, Prof. K.V. Sharma, Prof. V. Venkatachalam, Prof. S.V. Shastri and may others have been recognised as the notable personalities all over the world.

As such the study of Sanskrit, Indian languages and culture being presented as the form of modern Indological studies and researches, would be the torch bearer not only to the scholars of all the fields of India, but to that of the entire world. In a message therefore Mr. A.M. Khaleeli, the High Commissioner of India to Australia very well remarked in the eve of IX World Sanskrit Conference at Melbourne, in 1994, January that Sanskrit is one of the basic treasures of mankind fertilizing both directly and indirectly some of the finest movements of minds. He has clearly stated, Sanskrit and Sanskritic culture and literature have not only best expressed religious concepts and spiritual insights and constructed philosophical systems, but have inspired and enriched the metaphysical and methamatical vocabulary and contributed tremendous works in a wide range of fields such as astronomy, medicine, politics, poetics, linguistics and drama.

Now the need of Indological study and research is very well realised by the scholars of the world. In order to bring a standard in the progress of such awareness, attempts have been started since 1973 and in this year (ICO) International Congress of Orientalists was founded. Later on this organisation was named as International Congress for Asian and North African studies. This organization aimed at a number of fields like Egyptian Studies, Assyrian Studies, Iranian Studies, Indian Studies, South East Asian Studies, East Asian Studies, African Studies and so on. Gradually no doubt a lot of valuable contribution was made to potential

Indian studies in various sections. These contributions in one course helped to grow a feeling amongst the scholars to join hands together for Indian studies and about a century after the first International Sanskrit Conference in the name of *Vishva Sanskrit Sammelana* convened by the Government of India at New Delhi on 26-31, 1972. Next year the 29th (I.C.O.) conference was held in Paris where many scholars those who attended the conference at Delhi were present. There it was decided to establish a permanent organisation for Indological association which has been known as (IASS) International Association for Sanskrit Studies. Prof. V. Raghavan was elected there as President and Professor Ludwik Sternbach became the Secretary. The International Conference which was held in 1972 at Delhi was regarded as the first World Sanskrit Conference and the 9th World conference was held in 1994 in Melbourne, Australia. The 10th Conference was held in India. However, the other conferences for Sanskrit (World Sanskrit Conferences) were held in different parts of the world as follows.

II. Conference - at Torino - (Italy) 1975.
III Conference - at Paris - (France) 1977.
IV Conference - at Weimar - (Germany) 1979.
V Conference - at Vārāṇasī - (India) 1981.
VI Conference - at Philadelphia - (USA) 1984.
VII Conference - at Leiden - (Netherlands) 1987.
VIII Conference - at Vienna - (Austria) 1990.

It is interesting to note that the reputed universities like London, Harvard, Oxford etc. have not yet taken interest to hold this conference at their place which is still awaited by the scholars. The scholars who have taken keen interest in this world Sanskrit conferences would be remembered for ever. The pioneers and important personalities who have joined hands together with full interest in Indology are the following: Prof. R.N. Dandekar (India), Prof. Collette Caillat (France), Prof. S.Lienhar (Sweden), Prof. Oscar Botto (Italy), Prof. S. Iusler (USA), Prof. T.Y. Elizarenkova (Tussia), Prof. J.M. DE More (Mexico), Prof. M. Hara (Japan), Prof. W. Morgenroth (Germany), Prof. A.N. Aklujkar (Canada), Prof. G. Bailey, (Australia), Prof. C.A. DaFonseca (Brazil), Prof. J.C. Heesterman (Netherland), Prof. G. Obeyhammer (Austria), Prof. Asok Parpola (Finland), Prof. G Wojtilla (Hungary), Prof. Huangxin

Chuan (China), Prof. E. Bender (USA), Prof. R.K. Sharma (India), Prof. V. Raghavan (India) and many others. Besides these active members, a number of scholars from India and abroad are taking parts continuously in presenting valuable papers in these conferences discovering various key points in the Indological researches under eighteen disciplines like Vyākaraṇa, Linguistics, Modern Sanskrit Studies, Sanskrit and Computer, Vedic Studies, Epic and Purāṇic Studies, Āgama and Tantra, Kāvya, Hindu Studies, Buddhist Studies, Jaina Studies, Philosophy, Science and Medicine, History, Dharmashastra, Ritual, Art and Archaeology, and Study of Manuscripts.

Thus through modern Indological study and research the rich tradition of Indian civilization the then master minds handed down to us could have been properly investigated. This ultimately has been helpful to promote knowledge in all aspects of life and in various fields of learnings as practically found in different countries of the world.

BIBLIOGRAPHY

1. Mohapatra, G. *History of Sanskrit literature, preface,* Nalanda, Cuttack, 1994.
2. Mohapatra, G. Sanskrit and Culture, Ist Chapter, Published by Cultural Affairs Dept., Govt. of Orissa, 1975.
3. *Circulation Programme of IXth World Sanskrit Conference,* Melbourne (9th-15th, 1994), Melbourne, p. 8.
4. *News letter of the International Association of Sanskrit Studies, CESMEO, Torino, 1993.*

10

ASTRONOMY TO FIX THE DATES OF SANSKRIT TEXTS OR HISTORIC EVENTS

Vartak Padmakar Vishnu

For the study of History it is important to find out the date or at least a period of any incident in the history of any country. This aspect of fixing the dates of Indian history came to importance when European scholars began their studies of Indian history. The European scholars had no concept of measurement of Time with the help of Astronomy. They used to count the days and years from a particular king or event. Such records are not present in the ancient history of India. Therefore nobody was able to fix the dates of the ancient Indian history.

Lokamanya B.G. Tilak was the first scholar to search the Indian ancient history with the help of Astronomy. Studying his work I got inspiration to further his work. For that purpose I studied the time reckoning science of India. It made clear that the Indian authors have given details of time by the astronomical records and by proper studies we can easily fix the dates of various incidents in the ancient Indian history accurately.

We think that the modern scientific calender is very good because it is easy but it is not good. If a calender from our wall is lost we are unable to find the date and month. If we happen to go to some isolated island after wrecking our ship then in four to five days we will forget the date and month and then will never be recalled. But a man like me who has studied the Indian calender can easily tell *Tithi, Nakṣatra, Pakṣa,* Lunar month by looking at the night sky. By looking at the rising sun *Rutu* and *Ayana* can be told. Counting of the days can be done by Tithi and *Nakṣatra*. Tithi depends on the size and shape of the Moon. *Nakṣatra* is the star near which the moon is seen. Every day the moon changes its *Nakṣatra* and completes a round in 28 days. Thus the Indian calender is eternal.

Nakṣatra tells the position of the moon among the stars. *Tithi* tells the distance of the moon from the sun, because in one *Tithi* the moon goes 12 degrees away from the sun. Lunar month is named after the *Nakṣatra* near which the full moon resides. It is also the *Nakṣatra* which rises at the sun-set and remains visible throughout the night. From the name of the Lunar month the moon's position is fixed and from it the position of the sun can be easily calculated. The sun is exactly opposite at the full moon while both are together at *Amāvasyā*.

Rutus are six in number, three in each *Ayana*. *Ayanas* are two, *Uttarāyana* and *Dakṣināyana*. *Uttarāyana* means the Sun's northern journey. It begins with Shishira Rutu at the Winter Solstice on 22nd December of the modern calender. Dakshināyana is the southern journey of the sun which begins with the Varṣā Rutu at the Summar Solstice on 22nd June. Varsha, Sharad, Hemant are the three Rutus of *Dakshināyana*, while Shishira, Vasant and Greeshma are the three Rutus of Uttarāyana. Each Rutu consists of two solar months. Nabha and Nabhasya are the two solar months of Varsha Rutu which correspond with 22nd June to 21st July and 22nd July to 21st August. Isha and Urja are the two months of Sharad. Isha corresponds to 22nd August to 21st September. A period from 23rd September to 22nd October means Urja. 23rd Sept. or the beginning of Urja is the Autumnal Equinox having equal day and night. Hemant Rutu consists of Saha (22 Oct. to 21 November) and Sahasya (22 Nov. to 21 December). 22nd December is the Winter Solstice when Tapa, the first month of Rutu Shishira begins. The second month of Shishira i.e. Tapasyā extends from 22nd January to 21 February. Madhu, the first month of Vasanta Rutu begins on 22nd February and ends with the Vernal Equinox on 21st March. Then Madhava, the second month of Vasanta begins which ends on 21st April. From 22nd April Greeshma begins, the first month of which is Shukra. Its second month Shuchi begins on 22nd May and ends on 21 June. 22nd June is the Summer Solstice when Nabha and Varsha begin. Thus the solar seasonal months of Rutus correspond with the modern seasonal months. (*Taittirīya Saṁhita* 4.4.1. Also *Vishnu Purāṇa* Ansha 2, Adhyāya 8, Śloka 83)

Viṣṇu Purāṇa 2.8.70 clearly speaks about two solar months forming Rutu.

Ancient authors are particular to give *Tithi*, *Nakṣatra*, lunar month and Rutu. Sages are particular to mention the *Nakṣatra* of the Sun at the Winter Solatice or the Summer Solstice or the equinoxes. From these records it is evident that the ancient sages knew of the precession of Equinoxes due to which the Sun recedes in the Nakshatra Chakra. If we know the rate of the precession of equinoxes as one degree in 72 years or one Nakshatra in 960 years or one Rashi i.e. 30 degrees in 2160 years, we can calculate the year or the period of any incident about which these records are available. We get the data for calculations if the Rutu and lunar month is given, because the lunar month indicates the Sun's position in Nakshatras while Rutu indicates the Earth's position in relation to the Sun. Let us now see how precise is this method to fix the dates or years or period of some incidents.

Pancāṅga means five important points regarding the time. These are *Tithi*, *Nakṣatra*, *Māsa*, *Rutu* and *Ayana*. In addition to these five, the sages were particular to record the positions of the planets which pinpoint the time.

In the epic *Mahābhārata*, Maharshi Vyāsa gives the positions of all the planets in *Bhishma Parva*, Adhyāya 2,3, thus - Saturn in Pūrva, Jupiter in Sharvana, Rahu in Uttara Ashadha and Mars in Anuradhā. All these planets have a fixed rotational periods. Saturn completes one rotation in 29.4544832 years. Jupiter takes 11.863013 years for one rotation. Rāhu takes 18.5992 years, Mars takes 1.88089 years per rotation. Taking the respective positions of each of these planets in any year we can calculate backwards to find out when the planets were in the said positions. I found the year to be 5561 years before Christ. When Bhishma died it was Winter Solstice and he had fought for ten days and had lied on the arrowbed for 58 days. 68 days earlier that 22nd December is 16th October when the great war must have commenced. Thus we could fix the date of the *Mahābharata* war exactly as 16th October 5561 B.C., Three more planets are found decribed by Vyāsa in the *Mahābhārata* under the names of Shveta, Shyama and Teevra. These are Uranus, Neptune and Pluto. Calculating back we can find that the respective positions get confirmed on the above date. In addition Vyāsa describes two consecutive Amāvasyās, one Kshaya Paksha, two eclipses lunar and solar in one month's time and a big comet. All these evidences show the same date 16th October 5561 B.C. Eighteen mathematical points converge on this date and many other evidences point to the same date. Therefore we have to accept it as the date of the beginning of the *Mahābhārata* war.

Accepting this date we can fix the dates of about sixty incidents from the *Mahābhārata* including the date of exile 4th September 5574 B.C. and exposure of Arjuna on 16th April 5561 B.C.

Except Astronomy no other method can give such details and exact dates. In the case of the *Mahābhārata* we have to solve some riddles put forth by the sage Vyāsa deliberately, but in another books no such problem arises.

Rutus and lunar months as described in the *Mahābhārata* point to the same time of 5561 B.C. The planet Saturn had been in the arms of Rohiṇi according to the *Mahābhārata*. According to the calculations of late Shri Dixit S.B. this phenomenon took place for many centuries before 5294 B.C.

At the time of Rāma's birth five planets were exalted according to *Vālmiki Ramāyaṇa*. The exalted positions well-known in astrology are thus : Sun 10° in Mesha, Mars 28° in Makara, Jupiter 5° in Karka, Venus 27° in Meena, Saturn 20° in Tulā. For calculations of thousands of years only the slow moving planets are useful and only by two planets Saturn and Jupiter we cannot fix the exact date. At least three planets are essential. In the *Vālmiki Rāmāyaṇa* it is stated at Ayodhya Kāṇḍa 4/18 that the Sun, Mars and Rahu were aspecting Dasharatha's Nakshatra at the time of Rāma's coronation on Chaitra Shuddha 9th, when Rāma completed 17 years of his life. In the Chaitra māsa sun resides in Mesha Rāshi, so Rahu also must have been at Mesha or just opposite in Tulā Rāshi. Rahu completes one rotation in 18.5992 years, hence 17years earlier Rāhu must have been in Kanyā i.e. Virgo. Calculations on this data shows the date of Rāma's birth as 4th December 7323 years B.C.

Instead of coronation Rāma had to leave for forest in Hemanta Rutu on Chaitra Shuddha 9th. At this occasion Vālmiki states the star positions at Ayodhyā 41/10,11. These tally with the modern mathematics. Rāma went to the forest life on 29th November 7306 B.C. Rāma was married to Sītā on 7th April 73-7 B.C., in Bhadrapada Shuddha 3rd on Uttarā Phālguni Nakshatra.

When Hanumāna returned after burning Laṅkā, Vālmiki describes the sky vividly which indicates the date as Pousha Krishna 1st or 3rd September 7292 B.C. The war was fought from 3rd Nov. to 15th Nov. 7292 B.C.

I have fixed almost 40 dates of various important events from the *Rāmāyaṇa*, showing that the astronomical records are helpful in fixing dates in history.

Vedic literature records abundant astronomical data which can fix the periods. Ṛigveda 10161-13 states - "Who awakened Rubhus ? The Sun replied, 'The Dog, because today is the end of the year." The Dog means Canis major or Mruga Nakshatra. Rubhus means clouds. Clouds were awakened by Mruga means rains began with Mruga. At present rainy season begins with Mruga. Thus a cycle of 27 Nakshatras must have been elapsed between the present age and the Vedic age. At the rate of 960 years per Nakshatra 27 Nakshatras have taken 25920 years. So the Vedic statement is 25920 years old. In other word the period of Ṛgveda is 23720 years B.C.

Taittirīya Saṁhitā 7-4-8 states that Pūrva Phālguni is the last night of the year while Uttara Phalguni is the first night of the new year, and Vasanta is the mouth of the year. This shows the Vernal equinox in the month of Phālguna at the full moon. Naturally the Sun was diagonally opposite in the Bhādrapada Nakshatra at the vernal equinox showing a period of 23720 years B.C.

Ṛigveda 4-57-5 requests Shunasirau to shower the water made in heavens on the Earth. Shuna means god. Sirau means two heads. Two heads of dogs means Canis major and minor ine Mruga Nakshatra. This suggests beginning of the rainy season at Mruga Nakshatra the period being 23720 years B.C.

The quinoxes recede backwards through Nakshatras. So from Mruga it must have gone to Kṛttikā. To show it there is an evidence in the names of the stars of Kṛttikā. The constellation Kṛttikā is formed of seven small stars which are named as Ambā. Dulā, Nitatni, Abhrayanti, Meghayani, Varshayanti, Chuputikā. (*Taittirīya Brāhmaṇa* 3-1-4). All these names indicate water. Abhayanti means bringing Abhra i.e. white clouds. Meghayanti means bringing water-loaded black clouds. Varshayanti means bringing showers of rains. At the beginning of rainy season first white clouds or Abhra come, then Megha or water-loaded clouds come and then showers come. Thus these names definitely point to the rainy season. Kṛttikā was bringing the Varsha Rutu during 21800 years B.C.

Between Mruga and Kṛttika there is Rohiṇi. The rainy season must have began on Rohiṇi some time. It is reported in the *Mahābhārata* Vana Parva 230 wherein it is also stated that the fall of Vega or Abhijit began because Kṛttikās went to water i.e. Summer Solstice when Varsha Rutu began. This was the condition around 21800 years B.C. Before this during 22760 years B.C. the Summer solstice was at the Rohiṇi.

Apabharaṇi is a Vedic name of Bharaṇi Nakshatra. It was called as Apabharaṇi because it was filling water. How a Nakshatra from the sky fill water on the earth? Of course by inducing rains. Thus this name was given around 20840 B.C.

The deity of Mula Nakshatra is mentioned as Niruti. Nairutya means South-West. The sages discovered that the rainy season in India comes from south-west winds. Therefore they fixed the deity when Mula was at the summer solstice and introduced rains during 11240 B.C.

Before Mula, Purva Ashadha used to induce rains so that its deity is fined as Water during a period of 12200 B.C.

Ṛgveda 3-57-2 states "Indra and Poosha milch the clouds". Indra is the deity of Jyeshthā while Poosha is the deity of Revati. Thus the rainy season begins with Jyeshtha and ended with Revatī. This was during 10280 B.C.

Ṛgveda 1-164-19 states, "O Indra and Soma, you two rotating like a yoked horse are supporting this work." These rotating dieties are nothing else but the solstices. That time Jyeshthā was at the summer solstice whose deity is Indra, and Mruga whose deity is Soma was at the winter solstice. This period is 10280 B.C.

Taittirīya Brāhmaṇa 1-5-1-6,7 states that Kṛttikā to Vishākhā is the northern course of the Sun while Anurādhā to Āpabharaṇi was the southern course of the sun. This clearly shows that the winter solstice ws between Kṛttikā and Bharaṇi i.e. 26° 40′ while the summer solstice was between Vishākhā and Anurādhā at 213° 20′. On 22 December 1995 the sun is at 245° 50′ 45″ in Mūla Nakshatra on the winter solstice. It has come here from 26° 40′. So total shift back is 140° 49′ 15″. The rate of the precession of equinoxes is 50.2 per year. So it is seen that 10098. 704 years ago the statement is written. It comes to 8103 years B.C.

Āśrvalāyana Gṛyhya Sūtra 2-3-5 advises to meditate on Hemanta Rutu on Margashirsha Pūrṇimā. Naturally, Hemanta was ending at Magha Pūrṇimā on the winter solstice. The full moon at Māgha shows the sun to be at 307° at winter solstice. At present the winter solstice occurs at 246°. It shows that the sun has receded back by 61°. The precession rate is 72 years per degree. So 61 x 72 = 4392 years ago *Ashvalayana Gruhya Sūtra* is written. It shows 2404 B.C. at least 1900 B.C. as its period.

Sushruta Saṁhitā 6-10 tells rainy season in Bhādrapada and Ashvina Masas. It was the condition around 400 B.C. The Saṁhitā also states that Māgha Māsa and Shishira Rutu began together. This indicates 2000 B.C. Thus it appears that the first edition of Sushruta Saṁhitā was formed in 4000 B.C. while the second edition was prepared at 2000 B.C.

Maitrāyaṇi Upanishad 6/14 records the summer solstice at the beginning of the Māgha Nakshatra or at 120°. At present it is at 65° 40′ 42″. The difference is of 54° 19′ 18″ or 195558 seconds. The precession rate is 50.2″ per year. It shows that Maitrāyaṇi Upanishad is composed 3895.5776 years ago or 1909 B.C.

Vishnu Purāṇa tells at 2/8/66 to 76 that equal day and night come when the sun entered Mesha or Tula Rashi. It shows a period not later than 1609 B.C.

Vedānga Jyotisha shows the winter solstice on Dhanishthā which cannot be later that 1640 B.C.

Parashara tells Summer solstice at middle of Ashlesa at 113° 20′. Its date comes to 1159 B.C.

Kaushitaki or *Shankhayana Brāhmaṇa* 1/3 tells that in the middle of the rainy season one should see at the Punarvasu Nakshatra while offering oblation. But in these days in the fist fortnight the moon does not combine with Punarvasu. Therefore give oblation on Amavasya which comes after Āshaḍha, because on the Amavasya there is Punarvasu Nakshatra.

In the first fortnight Punarvasu is invisible in the months of Pausha to Āshaḍha. These are to be omitted. It shows that Jeshtha and Āshaḍha were not the months of rainy season. It is suggested to use Amavasyā coming after Āshaḍha. Thus it appears that the rainy season used to begin from Shravana masa. At present the rainy season begins from Jeshtha masa. The rainy season has shifted back by two months. It means that the sun has receded 60°. At the rate of 72 years per degree the shift must have taken place in 4320 years. Thus *Kaushitaki Brahmana* appears to be written around 2320 B.C.

Matsya Purāṇa 204/5 tells that if one oblates on the Trayodashi with Māgha Nakshatra during Varsha Rutu he gets benefitted. Māgha Nakshatra on Trayodhashi comes in Sharvana on Bhadrapada masa. Thus these two were the months of Varsha Rutu when *Matsya Purāṇa* is composed. The period is around 200 B.C.

Shrīmad Bhāgavata Purāṇa shows equal day and night when the sun was in Mesha or Tula Rashi. It shows the time to be 1600 to 2000 B.C.

Kālidāsa describes Varsha Rutu from Ashadha first day. From that he appears to be at the beginning of the Christian era i.e. 2000 years ago since today.

Varāhmihira gives the summer solstice at Karkadya i.e. at 90°. So his date is 520 A.D.

Thus all the steps of one to two thousand years are shown by Astronomy. This cannot be done by Archeology or linguistics or any other science or method. There is a gap from 12000 B.C. to 20000 B.C. which can be filled up by stray evidences such as the fall of Vega (Abhijit) mentioned in the *Mahābhārata* which took place around 13000 B.C. *Vālmiki Rāmāyaṇa* states that Daityakula had Mūla as their Nakshatra and Ikshvaku Kula Nakshatra was Vishakha. It means that Daitya Kula began when Vernal equinox was at Mūla i.e. 17000 B.C. Ikshvaku Kula started with Vishakha at the Vernal equinox around 15000 B.C. Thus King Bali, Hiranyakashipu etc. were ruling the earth around 17000 B.C. while Manu and Ikshavaku were living around 15000 B.C. Thus all the steps of history of the ancient Indian culture are seen ranging from 25000 B.C. to 520 A.D. Only Astronomy can give such fineries about time.

11

SOME NEGLECTED AREAS OF SANSKRIT RESEARCH

Sweta Prajapati

I. Introduction

In the National Policy on Education (NPE) 1986, great stress has been laid on research as an essential component of higher education because of its role in creating new knowledge and insights and imparting excitement and dynamism to the educational process.[1] Hence "all institutions of higher education must actively pursue research, and performance in research ought to be an important measure of success for the individual as well as the institution.[2] In this connection it is interesting to say that Sanskritists and the institutions of higher teaching and research of Sanskrit in India have, in fact, realised the value and utility of research and they have succeeded in producing commendable research works to a great extent. Consequently we witness a considerable amount of quantitative expansion of researches, especially doctoral researches in Sanskrit in various important areas of Sanskrit such as Vedic, Purāṇic, Philosophical, Literary and Linguistics etc. *Bibliography of Doctoral Dissertation* (1857-1970), published by Inter- University Board of India, now renamed as Association of Indian Universities (AIU), New Delhi, and BDD of 1974 keep updating the information. *The University News* of the AIU provides us weekly information and a clear picture of the substantial growth of doctoral researches in Sanskrit. From the reports of the above mentioned documents it is evident that the Sanskrit researchers have concentrated only on limited areas of Sanskrit and therefore they have made their doctoral investigations in the traditional and popular areas of Sanskrit research. We can categorise all those traditional areas of research as follows:

I. Vedic and Purāṇic
(including Brāhmaṇas, Upaniṣads, Sūtras and Post-Vedic Period)

II. Linguistics and Grammar

III. Poetics and Literary works
(Prose, Drama, Fiction, Poetry and History of Sanskrit Literature)

IV. Indian Philosophy

V. Manuscripts

All these areas of Sanskrit research are very important and essential. Hence critical investigation for exploring new facts and examining old ones in these areas and extension of the frontiers of the prominent branches of Sanskrit studies are quite necessary. Sanskritists should not ignore the importance of the emerging areas of Sanskrit research which have so far not been paid due attention.

We should realise the fact that the confinement of traditional areas of research gives rise to a number of problems. First of all, it creates scope for repetative studies and duplication. Secondly, it does not motivate to the Sanskrit researchers to work in the less explored and emerging areas on which future development of Sanskrit education is based. All these areas of Sanskrit research are also quite important and there is also scope for doing valuable research. So Sanskritists, to my mind, should not confine themselves only to those traditional areas of research. Since the society, because of the marvellous development of science and technology, is radically changed and socio-economic needs of individuals have been significantly changed, Sanskrit researchers should also pay their attention to the changing needs and demands of the present day society and carry out valuable research which will be relevant and directly related to the development of individual and society.

In this paper, therefore, I have made an attempt to focus on some emerging and important but less explored areas of Sanskrit research. I hope this will enlighten the young Sanskrit researchers and motivate them to undertake outstanding investigations in these important areas on which the future growth and development of Sanskrit to a great extent depends.

II. Study of Manuscripts

NPE (1986) in its report mentions about Indological research carried out in the Universities and Research Institutions. From its report it is known that research in Manuscriptology has not been taken up with any degree of seriousness in India. The Doctoral Bibliographies and the Reports of *University News* inform us about few studies which have been done in the most important areas of Sanskrit research i.e Manuscriptology. Manuscripts constitute most valuable source-books of Indian culture, Sanskrit language and Literature. The precious literature of Sanskrit is available in the form of Manuscripts which represent a tangible proof of the greatness and sublimity of Sanskrit Literature.

The great sublimity of contribution of Sanskrit literature made by the continued and persistent efforts of our philosophers, religious heads and scientists was handed down through the ages by means of handwritten Manuscripts which are immune from change, alteration and modification being source-books themselves. From the survey of the doctoral dissertations it is evidently clear that the doctoral students are not attracted to the work of edition and critical edition and study of Manuscripts. Only a few Ph.D. studies have been done. Day by day the number of Ph.D. students editing and publishing Sanskrit Manuscripts are becoming small. The reason appears to be that the editorial work involves hard labour and profound patience. Because the edition of a Manuscript involves intensive study of handwritten leaves, comparision of the text of one manuscript with the other copies of the same work, preparation of the press copy, noting the variant readings in foot-notes, preparation of indeces and appendices, preparation of an introduction, giving a summary of the book, details of manuscript material, the work and the author, supplied by the manuscripts. The edition is therefore, a very difficult and laborious process with scanty results, although the result in itself is of the highest value. The work also requires sound knowledge in Sanskrit especially Grammar which is also a very difficult subject. On the other hand to prepare a thesis based on an edited work or some Sanskrit works is less painstaking. A thesis can be compiled within six months, unless the subject is extremely diffcult and original, from other people's writings, and through such an endeavour a doctorate degree can be easily obtained. The work of the former class is not paying nor much appreciated while the latter although easier and cheaper brings greater gain in the form of degrees and emoluments. This is one of the reasons why the late Maharaha Sayaji Rao Gaekwad in his speech before the seventh session of the All-India Oriental Conference recommended that doctorate should be conferred on good editions of original works, and not merely on research compilations. It is certainly a fact that the researchers of Sanskrit do not realise the value of bringing out critical editions of rare and unpublished manuscripts. The result invariably is that there is more of second-hand and third-hand knowledge in existence to-day than original and first hand knowledge. As a matter of fact, our Ph.D. researchers are forgetting the difference between original research and compilation, and are concentrating more on compilations than on original material including manuscripts. The Ph.D. students also ignore the fact whether the topic undertaken for research is of any practical value to the present or future generation or are merely academic in character. In the domain of research original knowledge is that which is lost to humanity and is not available to the present generation. He is called an original worker who brings out this hidden knowledge from ancient source books and circulates amongst men for the first time. That is why greater respect is undoubtedly given to original workers and thinkers, than to scholars whose business is to compile information from other people's writings. The compilations undoubtedly have their own value, and those who find satisfaction in doing such works are welcome to do so, but this should not be encouraged in doctoral research stage lest the more difficult original work which increases our fund of knowledge may be neglected altogether. With lakhs of manuscripts unexplored it is not proper to waste our energies much on research and compilations, but to direct our attention solely to bring out editions of unpublished Sanskrit manuscripts. We should, therefore, create an environment which will inspire and encourage the young Sanskrit researchers to work on manuscriptology.

III. Interdisciplinary Approach

A recent emerging device of research named interdisciplinary approach is gaining much popularity in India. The importance of interdisciplinary approach for research cannot be denied in view of the changing social conditions not only in India but throughout the globe. The researchers have realised the fact that knowledge should not be imparted in piece meal. One subject cannot be completely isolated from the others. Such a knowledge is one side only and does not present comprehensive picture. Though the different disciplines differ among themselves, their areas are not completely different from each other i.e. they are correlated with one another through some common links. This is due to the fact that all the disciplines are centred around man's development common to all. This is why Kothari Education Commission (1964-66) opines "special efforts need also to be made to promote interdisciplinary studies in unversities which have adequately staffed departments in related subjects, new methods of co-operation between different institutions and new pattern of staffing.[3] NPE has also emphasised on interdisplinary research." To fulfil the need for the synthesis of knowledge, interdisciplinary research will be encouraged. Efforts will be made to delve into India's ancient fund of knowledge and to relate it to contemporary reality.[4] Report of the Sanskrit Commission (1956-1957) also gives stress on this approach of research.

Another new line of work which we may usefully adopt from America is the Interdisciplinary Study, where a specific general subject is studied and discussed by scholars belonging to different disciplines from different points of view, such as Language, Religion, Sociology, Economics and so on. This is of great help in developing a whole view of a subject. In Sanskrit there are several subjects which can be tackled like this from the points of view of different Śāstras. In connection with more general questions also, such as those pertaining to Indian Culture, institutions, etc., such an Interdisciplinary Seminar is bound to derive much light from the ideals and ideologies embodied in Sanskrit works.[5] Sanskrit researchers, therefore, try to conduct their researches by adopting interdisciplinary method.

IV. Computer and Use of Sanskrit Language

Truely speaking, we live in the age of computer. Recent years have witnessed the widespread acceptance of the significant role of computers in all works of human life. Computer has also created a revolution in the field of Sanskrit research.

Rick Briggs, an American computer scientist for the first time claimed; "Among the accomplishments of the ancient Indian grammarians can be reckoned a method for paraphrashing Sanskrit in a manner that is identical not only in essence but in form with the current work in AI (Artificial Intelligence)".[6] He further observed: "The Sanskrit grammarians have already found a way of solving what is perhaps the most important problem of computer science, namely, that of natural language understanding and machine translation."[7] Briggs made it clear in his article submitted in a revised version to the National Conference on Sanskrit and Computer held in Bangalore in Dec. 1986 that the Sanskrit which can be as an interlingua for the purpose of machine translation through knowledge representation is the Śastric Sanskrit. By Śastric Sanskrit he meant the language of *Śābdabodha* of the three schools - School of Grammar, Navya Nyāya school and Mīmāṁsā school. The grammarians' technique of varbal cognition developed by later grammarians like Kauṇḍabhaṭṭa and Nāgeśabhaṭṭa is compared by Briggs with the Semantic Net theory developed by modern computer scientists. He brought the fact that the extremely methodical and meticulous sentence analysis done by these grammarians as well as by the striking correspondence between the *Śābdhabodha* technique and the semantic net theory.

Subhash Kak, another computer scientist from Louidisna state University argues that Pāṇinian style generative rules and meta rules could assist in further advances in natural language processing. In his article entitled "The Paninian Approach to Natural Language Processing" Published in the *International Journal of Approximate Reasoning* (1987:1), Kak highly appreciates the Pāṇinian system of language analysis in the following words: "The greatest success of a constructive approach to the description of a natural language has ever had when Dākṣhiputra devised his grammar for the Sanskrit language".

Professor Kak pointed out with the help of illustrations how the Knowledge Representation Methodology in Pāṇinian grammar is in many ways equivalent to the more powerful currently researched artificial intelligence schemes. Finally, Kak suggested two ways to obtain a successful extraction of knowledge by overcoming the difficulty posed by the intrinsic ambiguity of a natural language: (1) Use of Sanskrit as an intermediary natural language, and (2) to seek new generative, Pāṇinian style of grammar for the English language.

From the above it becomes clear that it is an emerging and important area of Sanskrit research. The Ph.D. researchers should endeavour to work in this new field so that some valuable result will come out.

V. Ancient Sciences

In Sanskrit research the areas like Yoga, Āyurveda and other technical sciences are of paramount importance. This subjects being directly related to human life are in demand in the present day society. Since the human life gets much more benifited by the study of these subjects Sanskrit researchers should undertake their valuable investigations in these areas. But it is a matter of great regret that these areas are quite neglected. A survey of research studies reveal about the limited amount of research that has been done in these areas. Similarly the subjects like Jyotiṣa, Tantra and other subjects are also neglected. It is known that the studies which has been pursued at the doctoral level don't cover various aspects of these sciences.

VI. Sanskrit Education

We live in a period of exceptionally rapid change in all sectors of our social life. Sanskrit Education as a sub-system of society cannot escape the impact of this change. So Sanskritists must reflect to consider the innovation approaches to meet the challenges of future. This is both inevitable and essential as societies are faced with new problems, social, economic, political and environmental. Educational institutions are undergoing educational and social revolution. Research indicates that individual students do not have a similar type of educational standard, they no longer need old text-books, the old and traditional method of teaching and old curricular programme. They need different types of instruction and modern methods of teaching and need to be exposed to various instructional materials. Sanskritists should consider seriously these factors and try to innovate new ideas and practices and solve the problems they face in different areas of Sanskrit education such as methods of teaching in Secondary education and Higher education of Sanskrit, curriculum, needs and problems of the students. Educational changes, if they are to be successfully carried out, need to be based on research experimentation and a try-out of new ideas. Deliberation and dialogue, research and extension, thinking and dissemination, are rightly regarded as appropriate and effective techniques for the revitalization of the Sanskrit education renewal-movement. Keeping in view the dynamic nature of Sanskrit education research in its various aspects becomes necessary to sustain freshness and to add to the store of existing knowledge. The area is vast and research is necessary in nearly all aspects of Sanskrit. Keeping in view the emerging new trends in Sanskrit education and also to face challenges in the 21st century there is a great need for research in Sanskrit education. For this purpose a serious exercise in the direction of fixing up priorities of research in the area of Sanskrit education is needed. It may be wroth-while to give direction to the researchers, the type of researches to be taken up in India in future.

In the following pages a few areas in Sanskrit education for research are suggested:

1. There is an urgent need to undertake research problems on different methods of Sanskrit education. It is because of the fact that in the present age the students no more find interest in the traditional method of teaching Sanskrit. With the advancement in science and technology, the traditional lecture method by and large adopted by Sanskrit teachers is not suited. The present-day scientists' age calls for a variety of approaches to teaching in order to achieve different instructional objectives. We need research, therefore, to innovate and find out the best method to achieve the goal.
2. Research on developing and preparing the effective curriculum keeping in view the socio-economic and professional needs of the learners and the new trend in curriculum construction is needed.
3. Another area of research which requires immediate attention is to find out ways and means by which we can make Sanskrit education effective and interesting. This is directly related to the teaching aids and modern-day techniques etc., which motivate the students to physical and mental activity and to make teaching concrete, effective and interesting.
4. As Sanskrit teacher is the pivot in every scheme of work, one of the areas of research, therefore, could be the research on various aspects of Sanskrit teacher's training programme i.e. curriculum, how to develop attitudes, aptitudes, abilities, up- date knowledge, inservice programme, involvement of teachers in policy framing etc.
5. Evaluation, either external or internal occupies an important place in any system of education. The importance of any reasonable

method of evaluating the academic performance of the students cannot be ignored. There is need to study comprehensively the factors which are standing on the way of the implementation of the reforms in evaluation of Sanskrit students.

6. There is an immediate need to explore the mental level of the students, their interests, aptitudes, potentialities who are interested for Sanskrit education. We should also try to study the effects of different mediums on the students.

7. The areas of research which require special attention is the preparation of question papers. To study the problems related to the preparation of question papers and suggest remedial measures is quite important.

VI. Conclusion :

In this paper I tried to indicate the important and emerging areas of Sanskrit research. Since all these areas are not studied thoroughly our researchers should utilise their energy in exploring and experimenting the ancients' fund of knowledge. Study of these areas will, undoubtedly help the development of individual and society.

REFERENCES

1. Government of Indian Ministry of Human Resource Development, Department of *Education, National Policy on Education 1986 (NPE) Programme of Action* 1992, New Delhi, p. 86.
2. *Ibid.*
3. *Report of the Kothari Education Commission* (1964-66), Ministry of Education, Government of India, New Delhi, The Manager of Publication Division, 1966, p. 319.
4. NPE- 1986 p. 26.
5. Briggs, Rick. 1985, Knowledge Representation in Sanskrit and Artificial Intelligence, *The Aii Magazine,*, spring.
6. Briggs, Rick 1986, *Shastric Sanskrit in Interlingua for Machine Translation,* paper presented in the First National Seminar on 'Knowledge Representation and Sanskrit', Bangalore, December, 1986.

12

DOCTORAL RESEARCH IN SANSKRIT : SOME REFLECTIONS

Rabindra Kumar Panda

Introduction

During the past two decades a surprising amount of doctoral research studies leading to the degree of Ph.D has been done by the Sanskritists in the field of Sanskrit in India. It has increased enormously in the last decade and is increasing significantly as it is evident from the reports of the *University News* published by the Association of Indian Universities. The available data of the research undoubtedly creates an illimitable pleasure. Though Sanskrit has a little practical utility in the present age still the academic interest in this dicipline is increasing, consequently the doctoral research in Sanskrit is also growing. Though it happens from a multiplicity of standpoints and perspectives still it is not well-come. But the problem which raises its head and creates an alarming situation is the phenomenal quantitative growth in the volume of doctoral research and because of the quantitative expansion, the aspect of the quality is suffering a good deal. Unprecedented spurt of the doctoral studies obscure concern for quality and as a consequence of this trend, except in a few exceptional cases, the output of work is marked by mediocrity and poor quality. As a result of this, the highest academic degree, Ph.D is becoming very cheap and unpopular.

Mainly two aspects of the doctoral research in Sanskrit have serious concern. One is academic quality and the other is relevance from social point of view. It is a matter of great regret that there has been a steady deterioration in all aspects of doctoral research in Sanskrit. The standard maintained by the forerunners in the discipline and which is expected from the highest academic degree concerning the novelty of the problem or topic contributing significantly to the existing stock of knowledge in the area, treatment of the problem, methodology and language etc. is seriously falling. As far as my knowledge is concerned, only a few doctoral research are of expected and appreciable standard but a large number of research are of very inferior type and valueless. These studies no way contribute to the existing stock of knowledge because these are purely made for getting a degree and thereby achieving either a job or a professional promotion. Since the concern of quality has taken a back seat and relevance aspect is not taken care of seriously, a mass of worthless books have been produced in the name of academic research. As far as I can see, this unwanted and unproductive growth is because of some of the important factors namely, the problem of unemployment, professional promotion of guiding teachers and craze for cheap degree to enhance social prestige. These factors are not in need of elaboration. But what I want to emphasise is the fact that because of these goals the research is becoming just a mechanical preparation devoid of valuable exploration and significant contribution. As the process becomes very easy and less painstaking there is a mad rush after Ph.D. degrees in the various university-departments. Those who are jobless are endeavouring to achieve the Ph.D. degree in less time and easiest manner because preference is given to the Ph.D. degree at the selection of the post of a lecturer in a college or University. Those who have already been Lecturers are in a hurry to obtain the Ph.D. degree for their promotion by short-cut methods. The research guides are very busy in adding scores to their names, because production of each Ph.D. may add one additional feather to their caps. During the last two decades we have large number of registered Ph.D. scholars in the field of Sanskrit research in India. As a result of the mad rush doctoral research suffers from serious inadequecies. If research is defined as a scientific process for acquiring new knowledge or making an advancement of existing knowledge, even a cursory review of recent whole mass in the area of Sanskrit research may be found extremely disappointing as most of the research has been just repetitive, muddying the water rather than cleaning confusions.

Another aspect which causes serious concern is the relevance of the doctoral research. The type of research that is being done in the departments of Indian Universities does not seem to be very much relevant to the present society. Relevance needs to be attended to in the changed social context in India. This is why much of Sanskrit research has lost its credibility being devoid of proper perspective, clear objective and adequate rationale and therefore it fails to make any worth while contributing to the knowledge of the discipline.

Quality Deterioting Causes

The important point to note is that the most of the doctoral research in Sanskrit is of repetitive nature. Somebody has done a pioneer work in a particualr area which could be claimed as original. But afterwards a number of persons have conducted similar studies with a little modification here and there but with no improvement of content of any kind. But why such repetitions occur? We cannot simply blame the research-students for this. The factor which is responsible for this is the want of a survey of doctoral research in Sanskrit done in Indian Universities. So far the world of the Sanskrit scholars is not able to prepare a survey which will provide detailed information about number, type, trend, and areas of research in Sanskrit. It is therefore difficult in the part of a student-researcher and guide to know the topics or problems on which studies have been made and to identify a new problem of research. There is no other direct source also to know about the studies. The journal known as 'Prachijyoti published by the university of Kurukshetra was publishing a list of the topics on which Ph.D. works were done and topics registered for Ph.D. Unfortunately now it is not regular.

Since we do not have a systematic survey of the research studies the process of evaluation of Ph.D. theses made by external referees are also gets affected. The experts also find difficulty in pointing out the duplication or plagiarism or manipulation of the data by the research students.

The absense of a critical survey also creates grave problem for the student researcher on his way of making a critical review of the related literature of the related Ph.D. theses done in a paticular area, or a theory or a topic. By making a review one becomes able to know about the existing position of knowledge and can think of the advancement of the knowledge. Hence for Ph.D. students in Sanskrit there is no scope to think and plan for the advancement of knowledge in general.

Secondly, the language of writing a research thesis is an important factor which significantly contributes for the deterioration of quality. For Sanskrit research a number of languages or mediums like English, Sanskrit, Hindi, Gujarati, Marathi etc. are followed by the departments of the universities, Sanskrit Viswavidyalayas, Sanskrit Vidyapeethas and Oriental Research Institutes. This leads to repetition. One gets oppertunity to collect a Ph.D. work in any language, say English, makes a little change and presents it in a different language. Whatever changes they try to bring in is simply an alteration in nomenclature or title, in the arrangement of the chapters and language.

The third disappointing factor is the want of a stnadard research methodology for a unique discipline like Sanskrit. This is why both the student-researchers and guides face a lot of difficulties about the research process which includes the following steps viz. selection of the research problem, techniques of collecting data and interpreting, analysing data, presentation of the findings, reporting etc. But this aspect of Sanskrit research is mostly neglected by the reserchers which needs greater attention. To improve the quality of these aspects research methodology is quite important and regarding research methods some hard thinking is necessary. Another worth-mentioning point is that doctoral studies in Sanskrit hardly indicate about their objective of the study, plan and procedure, rationale, review of related literature and findings etc. which are absolutely inevitable while reporting. In order to set standards in doctoral researches, the appropriate use of different methodologies of research and appropriate use of various modern scientific techniques are to be employed.

Fourthly, the factor which causes the deterioration of the quality is the lack of proper training of the fresh young researchers who just after passing their post-graduate degree register for the Ph.D. They are not given any training about how to carry out research in a scientific manner. But for them a course of training is quite essential. The students who are coming for Ph.D. after the completion of M. Phil. their case is different since they get training both in theory and practice by studying the books on research methodology and by writing a dissertation on the subject in the particular sub-area of the discipline. But for the fresh post-graduates reseach training is must because a paper/course on Research Methodology is absent in the existing M.A. syllabi. Simply guidance of a supervisor or a guide is not sufficient. This not only affects academic standards of doctoral research but also affects the psycho-physical aspects of researchers by creating mental tensions, worries and anxieties about what to do and how to do etc. It also consumes their valuable time because of their ignorance of the means for the achievement of them. When the process is faulty how can we expect a product to be faultless. National Policy on Education (NPE) in para 37 rightly endorses:

> Apart from the fact that the quality of research undertaken in universities and institutions of higher learning in humanities leaves much to be desired, research in manuscripts and materials available in Sanskrit, Pali and Prakrit, old Tamil and other classical languages has not been taken up with any degree of seriousness in India, particularly with a view to establish the validity and relationship of the knowledge and experience embeded in these languages to contemporary scientific thought and technological development.

Taking into consideration the fact noted by the NPE, our Ph.D. researchers should not confine themselves to the popular and traditional areas of research. They should pay due attention to the manuscripts, as the content, value and standards of the research work in the field of Sanskrit primarily depend on the discovery of outstanding Sanskrit works among the manuscripts lying scattered all over the country.

NPE has also emphasised the need for research in Sanskrit in the field of Indology particularly with a view to "delving into India's ancient fund of knowledge and to relate it to contemporary reality". This effort will imply the development of facilities for the intensive study of Sanskrit". NPE has encouraged and promoted interdisciplinary research in Sanskrit and Indology to fulfill the need for the synthesis of knowledge. The Sanskritists, therefore, should be assiduous to conduct and inspire research in emerging areas like interdisciplinary , multidiciplinary etc.

Our Ph.D. scholars should also attempt to study the common features of the classical languages from cultural perspective. NPE has also proposed for the establishment of an international institute at the time of formulating the seventh five year plans. The objectives envisaged were to enable scholars to find the roots of a common world culture in Indian and foreign classical literature. The classical languages like Sanskrit, old Tamil etc., have several common features and a study of these would not only help to project Indian culture but also enrich modern ideas and concepts.

There are other factors also which are though less significant, still stand on the way of academic quality and desirable Ph.D. standard. A few of them is mentioned.

It is observed that in the entry level of Ph.D., no such strict and regorous scrutiny of the candidates, academic qualifications, their class, percentage etc. is done. The system has become so loose that there is no bar at all for doing Ph.D. and any body therefore can register for Ph. D. just after possessing a post- graduate degree. Consequently the students who have not secured 55% of marks in their M.A. degree and not eligible even for the post of a lecturer, also register and try to get a Ph.D. degree by hook or crook. Since some guides do not get students or in a hurry to get promotion allow such students. This trend should be stoped. It should be considered that Ph.D. is not everybody's cup of tea.

As far as the present writer is informed, there are some institutions which do not follow the criteria of minimum two years duration for the submission of Ph.D. thesis. There is no strict rule that one should work minimum for two years after registration for submission. Taking advantage of this situation, Ph.D. guides and Ph.D. students produce useless works under the name of Ph.D. research in the shortest possible time. These institutions should be identified and punished so that we can expect the academic standard.

Thirdly, the system in which a registration of Ph.D. is done is farcical and quite unbearable. Before knowing what research is, students get registered themselves for Ph.D degree just being given topics by enthusiastic guides. This is not good at all. Before registration a student should spend at least some months in studying the literature in a particular area, should prepare an independent proposal of research, should present his proposal before the staff-members of the department and should appear the interview. If he becomes successful in all these stages he should be allowed to register for Ph.D.

Fourthly, there should be strict evaluation of Ph.D. studies by the external experts who in some cases come under the influence and approach of guides and submit the favourable reports in the case of useless works. The process of evaluation should be regorous and due recognition should be given to quality only.

Conclusion

This aforegoing discussion leads to the conclusion that quality control in doctoral researches in Sanskrit is thus not only important but very urgent. The current trend of diluting quality for the sake of quantity needs to be arrested and quality in research resorted if the discipline of Sanskrit has to have a measure of respectability and status as an academic discipline. There is an urgent need in this country for taking up research in Sanskrit which has a definite social objective and is relevant to our present-day needs, and whose results can be generalised over a reasonably large population.

Doctoral research in Sanskrit suffers from many shortcomings and maladies. Effrots have to be made to devise ways and means of eradicating these defects and solve the long standing problems. Considering the special importance of Sanskrit to the growth and development of Indian languages and its unique contribution to the cultural unity of the country Sanskrit research should receive high priority. To improve the quality and check the deterioting trends of doctoral researches we should arise, awake and act. The following suggestions may be taken into consideration for the improvement of the condition.

1. A critical Survey of doctoral researches done in the Universities and Institutions is to be prepared.
2. Two or three mediums of reportings or writing - Sanskrit, Hindi or English - are to be allowed.
3. A standard research methodology especially for Sanskrit research is to be worked out.
4. Due attention is to be given to the important areas like manuscripts etc.
5. A rigorously selective approach has to be adopted.
6. Critical and impartial evaluation of the researches is necessary.
7. Studies are to be conducted in the comparatively less explored and non-traditional/popular areas like (1) Teaching Methods of Sanskrit (2) Curriculam (3) Training of Sanskrit Teachers.

REFERENCE

1. Government of India, Ministry of HRD, Department of Education, *National Policy on Education 1986 - Programme of Action*, New Delhi.

13

TIBETOLOGY AND THE INDOLOGICAL STUDIES

Narendra Kumar Dash

The Tibetan historians have unanimously accepted that literacy began in Tibet with the introduction of Buddhism in their country. The famous King Sron-btson-gam-po of the Tibetan Royal Empire married the princess of China and Nepal to keep good contact with these two neighbouring countries. Furtunately both these two princess were staunch follower of Buddhism or the *Buddha-Dharma*. They requested the king to build two separate temples (Tib. lha-khang) for the images of lord Buddha, those were taken with them from their own countries. The king agreed with them and ordered to build the temples. Thus Buddhism entered into Tibet for the first time during the reign of the said king i.e. in the mid-seventh century A.D. Though Buddhism entered into Tibet during this period still it was actually spread over Tibet in the eighth century A.D., when the famous Indian Paṇḍits like Padmasaṁbhava, Śāntarakṣita and Kamalaśila visited Tibet to teach the secrets of Buddhism in the land of snow.

Sron-btson-gam-po advised his minister Thon-mi-Sambhota to visit India to learn Indian scripts and the Sanskrit language. He came to India and learned the Indian alphabetes from *Lipikāras* and the Sanskrit language from Devavidyāsiṁha in Kashmir. Later a good number of Indian Paṇḍits also visited Tibet. Again the poineers of Buddhist religion and culture in Tibet had their own training in India presumably at some Buddhist monasteries. The Tibetan script was based on the Indian scripts, the Tibetan Grammar on Indian grammar, perhaps on the *Aṣṭādhyāyī* of Pāṇini. Throughout the subsequent history of Tibet, education remained primarily Buddhist. Knowledge of Buddhism was the highest mark of Tibetan learning. Translation of an Indian text under the guidance of one or two more Indian Paṇḍits was the peak of academic ambition for a Tibetan scholar.

Thus, with the joint efforts of the Indian and Tibetan scholars so many important works in Sanskrit language were translated into Tibetan language. Some of the translation works are as the original Sanskrit works are not available in India at present.

Before a discussion on the works those were translated into Tibetan from Sanskrit, we would like to say some words about the procedure of the translation activities in Tibet. The translation of the texts were done in a scientific way. In some cases the earlier translations were revised to give an uniformity. It is known from the history that the Thirty-third king of the Tibetan Royal Empire had constituted a committee for the translation of the Buddhist Sanskrit works comprising of Indian and Tibetan scholars. It is also known that in the said committee at least fifty percent members were from India. The Tibetans also did not forget to compose a Dictionary type of work containing the original Sanskrit technical words of various subjects and their Tibetan equivalents. This very work entitled the *Mahāvyutpatti* helped much to the latter translators who were engaged to translate the Sanskrit works into Tibetan. It is to mark that some Tibetan *Lotasabās* also have consulted the Chinise translation of a text to remove their doubts on some difficult passages. Thus the translation of the Sanskrit works in Tibet was very systematic.

The history of the translation activities in Tibet shows that the Buddhist Sanskrit works and other important works of India were translated into Tibetan in three phases. The first phase of translation activities was confined within late seventh century A.D. to early tenth century A.D. Towards the end of the first phase the last king of the Tibetan Royal Empire, Lang Dar-ma was assassinated by Lha-lung Pal-dar. Lang-dar-ma persecuted and suppressed Buddhism in the land of snow. Then the holy *dharma* and the translation of the works connected with this was stopped. The second phase became alive only after the visit of the great Indian scholar, Dīpaṁkara Śrījñāna or Atīśa. There was no central rule in Tibet when Atīśa visited Tibet. The local chieftains helped much for the translation of the Buddhist and other secular works into Tibetan from Sanskrit, Pali and Chinese. Some of the works were also translated into Mongolia Language during this second phase. The majority of the works were translated during this period. Only after the introduction of the Lamaism in Tibet, the third phase of translation activites was began. The great Sanskrit scholar, fifth Dalai Lama inspired for the translation of important Buddhist and other Sanskrit works. The *sūtras* of Pāṇini and other four commentaries on it were translated into Tibetan only during this phase. It is interesting to note that the *sūtras* of Candragomin, the *Kalpa Vyākaraṇa* and the *Sāraswata* were translated into Tibetan before the translation of the *sūtras* of Pāṇini.

The Chinese scholars had translated the Buddhist texts from the original Sanskrit in the second century A.D. onwards, but the Tibetans made most outstanding contributions through preserving the Sanskrit texts in literal and accurate translations, in which they surpassed the Chinese in accuracy and Volume. Therefore, for a good and thorough study on Indolgy we need the help of the Tibetan works. Hence knowledge of Tibetan Language is essential for a good scholar on Indology. Again, the Tibetan language contains the richest collection of Buddhist literature in the world to-day. All aspects of the Buddhist tradition-Hinayāna, Mahāyāna and Vajrayāna are contained within its scope.

Scholars have classified the Tibetan literature into two broad divisions: Religious and Non-religious. The religious literature can be classified in two ways i.e. (a) according to origin, and (b) according to subject. In the first group, a large number of works were translated from Indian sources into Tibetan. Besides, there is the enoromous Volume of religious works written by Tibetan scholars. The non-religious works also may be divided like the previous One. Bstan-'gyur texts, whose subject matter is mainly non-religious, include sixty-seven treatises on logic, twenty on grammar, seven on medicine, eighteen on art and fifty- seven on other subjects.

Now we would like to mention the names of some works which have been translated into Tibetan. The works of Pāṇini, Cāndra, Saptavarman and Anubhuti-svarūpācārya have been preserved in the translation form in Tibetan alongwith some commentaries on the said works. There is a vast poetic literature in the Tibetan translation. They are *Kavyādarśa* by

Daṇḍin and the *Meghadūtam* of Kālidāsa. Some Tibetans have also written some commentaries on the *Kavyādarśa*. They are Panglo Jamyang Khache, Rinpungpa, Pawo, Fifth Dalai Lama, Podkhepa, Minling Lochen, Khampa Chokyi Nyima, Mipham Namgyal and Kunzang Tendzin.

The metrical work *Chandoratnākara* of Ratnākara-śāntipāda is also translated into Tibetan. The Lexicons like *Amarakośa*, the *Kāmadhenu* and the *Abhidhānamuktāmālā* have been translated from Sanskrit. In the field of Logic all most all the works of Diṅnāga, Nāgārjuna, Dharmakīrti and Śāntarakṣita are preserved in the translation form in Tibetan. Many works on astrology, Mathematics, law, medicine, geography, dance and music, arts and crafts and political writings have been translated.

Now we would like to end this small paper with the comment that Indological studies is not complete without the study of Tibetology and therefore Indian Universitis and Research Institutions should make arrangements to study Tibetology alongwith Indological Studies.

14

ALAṄKĀRAŚĀSTRA: AN IMPORTANT FIELD OF RESEARCH IN SANSKRIT

Preeti Adhiya

I. Introduction :

Among all the Śāstras in the field of Sanskrit literature, Alaṅkāraśāstra, to my mind, is most interesting and important. Unlike other difficult Śāstras such as Navya-Nyāya, Mīmāṁsā and Vyākaraṇa etc., Alaṅkāraśāstra is comparatively easy and accessible to the students of average merit. It is a sukumāraśāstra and meant for *sukumāramatis*, (persons of delicate mind). But it does not mean that the Alaṅkāraśāstra is less important than the other Śāstras in Sanskrit. Eminent rhetoricians like Ānandavardhana, Abhinavagupta, Mammaṭa, Jagannātha and others have brought to Sanskrit poetics the same status and dignity as that of Sanskrit Grammar and principal systems of Indian philosophy like Vedānta. In quantity too, poetics vies with any other science or system of philosophy in Sanskrit. The subject matter of Alaṅkāraśāstra is very interesting for it deals with the nature of Kāvya and its various aspects like Rasa, Dhvani, Alaṅkāra, Guṇa, Rīti, Doṣa and above all the beauty of Kāvya as well as the process of beautifying the Kavya. The Alaṅkāraśāstra is, therefore, known by the various names viz. Sāhityavidyā, Saundaryaśāstra, Saudaryamīmāṁsā, Kāvyaśāstra etc.

II. Relevance

It is here necessary to speak few words about the relevance of the Alaṅkāraśāstra, when I particularly deal with the needs and problems of research in the field of Alaṅkāraśāstra. Now, the most important question which confronts serious researchers of our time especially in the context of development or advancement of knowledge, is: What is the relevance of the research in Sanskrit in general and Alaṅkāraśāstra in particular. We should not forget that the knowledge is not for the sake of knowledge. It should be useful for the development either of man or the society. Even our traditional thinkers and philosophers are of the view that knowledge is having the nature of illuminating. It illuminates the new objects and takes us from the field of ignorance to light and pleasure. Analysing from this point of view, the research, we are concerned with, is a knowledge generating process and so the knowledge generated by the research should lead us to light which will be useful for overall development of human beings. Otherwise there is no point either in studying the subject or making any research on it by spending a lot of money and precious energy.

With this background in view, when we ponder over the question of relevance of the Alaṅkāraśāstra at present time we get a positive and a definite answer. Yes, it is relevant, at least from two points of view. One, Alaṅkāraśāstra is a tool of creating new literature. For the persons who want to be poets or writers or want to create literature of any kind, the study of the Alaṅkāraśāstra is simply unavoidable. Without understanding properly, what a Kāvya is and what is its process of creating and what are the things by which a Kāvya arrests the hearts of connoisseur and what are the things which makes a Kāvya ugly, one cannot simply proceed in the work of composition and if he starts composing he simply becomes a laughing stock, as very rightly said by the great poeticians.

Secondly, some of our poeticians have composed independent works and some have devoted some portions in their works also about the method of *kāvyanirmāṇa*. As the study of existing works of Sanskrit literature is important so also the creation of the new literature in the field of Sanskrit is important. It is important for the development of Sanskrit language and its literature.

I must say with confidence that because of the negligence of Alaṅkāraśāstra, the standard of Sanskrit poetry and other literature is not properly maintained.

Alaṅkāraśāstra is also relevant to evaluate the works of literature created from time to time. The entire system of Sanskrit poetics is concerned with the process of evaluation. It has developed some systematic techniques for the evaluation of works of art by analysing its essential parts like *Guṇa, Doṣa* etc., as a physician examines a physical body and comes out with the conclusion of its soundness and defects.

III. Scope of the Alaṅkāraśāstra

Prof. H. Jacobi in his work, *Zeitchrift der Deutschen Morgen Laṅdischen Gesellschaft*, IVI p. 498 fn.1 in 1902, marked the scope of Alaṅkāraśāstra and brought into the currency the term poetics with reference to it for the first time. He enlightend us the vast scope of Alaṅkāraśāstra. As far as my knowledge is concerned, this has not been realised fully by the researchers of our time. Sanskrit Alaṅkaraśāstra inspite of its name, possesses a speculative interest by involving, besides mere rhetorics, a great deal of what is known today as criticism or aesthetics. No doubt, a good amount of study and research has been done in this important field by the enthusiastic and dedicated scholars, yet there is a vast land which needs investigation and exploration.

IV. Critical Edition of Important Alaṅkāra Works

In a country like India, rich in glorious traditions of ancient cultures and civilization, which had been the envy of the world, it is expected that one inclined towards exploration and diligent research is likely to come across numerous wreckages and remains of ancient learning. If one branch of Archaeology consists in unearthing past-remains of hoary antiquity, another direction in which our endeavour could be profitably diverted is to bring out from the darkness of oblivion and neglect valuable manuscripts of ancient learning into the light of publicity for the benifit of the whole modern world of savants and scholars. In the field of Alaṅkāraśāstra, many more important works, especially of the post-Jagannātha period, are still lying in the manuscript form in different manuscript libraries of India and Abroad. They have not so far seen the light of the day. To name a few, Pradhānavyaṅkamātya's *Alaṅkāramaṇi-darpaṇa,* Kulluri Rājaśekhara's *Alaṅkāramakaranda,* Kāśilakṣmaṇa Kavi's *Shāhabhūpālaṅkāra, Alaṅkāraśaṅkara* of Śaṅkara, *Alaṅkārasūryodaya* and *Alaṅkārarāghava* of Yajñeśwaradīkṣita and so on.

Apart from these important works, there are hundreds of minor works on Sanskrit poetics dealing with a particular aspect either of *Rasa* or of *alaṅkāra*, or of *Sabdavṛttis*. They are also existing in the form of manuscripts. What to talk of commentaries? A good number of valuable commentaries are still eating dust under the selves of the closed and dark rooms of the manuscript libraries. The present researcher who is preparing a Ph.D. thesis on the topic - *'Alaṅkāra Works of Naiyāyikas: A Study'* came to know in course of her investigation that there are more than hundred commentaries only written on the *Kāvyaprakāśa* of Mammaṭa. The Śāstrakāras like Naiyāyikas, Vaiyākaraṇas, Mīmāṁsakas, Tāntrikas and Jains have written commentaries. A few of them have been published; a few of them have been critically edited; and a few of them are available in print. Similarly, there are many valuable commentaries written on the important works like *Alaṅkārasarvasva, Kāvyādarśa, Sāhityadarpaṇa* etc. If our researcher-friends will develop interest in preparing the critical editions of those important orginal texts and commentaries, they will be able to make valuable contributions to this field of Alaṅkāraśāstra. There is, in fact a need of such hard and strenuous efforts.

V. Study of Alaṅkāra Works in their Relation to Other Śāstra Works

It is true that many research works have been done on various aspects of Kāvyaśāstra like *Rasa, Dhvani, Rīti* etc. As we see Alaṅkāraśāstra has been enriched by borrwings of the theories, concepts and thoughts from other Śāstras like Vyākaraṇa, Mīmāṁsā and Navya-Nyāya. Some of the Śāstrakāras belonging to their respective Śāstras especially the Naiyāyikas and Mīmāṁskas have also interpreted some of the poetic theories and concepts from the point of view of their Śāstras. The study of such works and such interpretations will open up new vistas in the field of Sanskrit poetics. The works of research like Alaṅkāraśāstra and Nyāyaśāstra, Alaṅkāraśāstra and Mīmāṁsā, Alaṅkāraśāstra and Vyākaraṇa, Alaṅkāraśāstra and Vedānta could be prepared by the young and enthusiastic research scholars and give us the valuable fruits of their investigations. Similarly, works on the contributions of the Buddhists and Jains should be taken up.

VI Comparative Studies of Indian Literary Theories with Western Literary Theories

Among other areas which require research one is the comparative field. There is the need of comparative studies of Indian literary theories and concepts with their Western counterparts. As in the case of Indian philosophy, Indian religious systems etc., so in the case of Indian literary criticism also, there is a necessity of comparative studies of Indian literary theories including aesthetics with the Western theories of aesthetics, stylistics and linguistics. These will open new avenues of research by way of correlating the ideas of the literary critics of India with those of Western literary theorists. The works like the correlation between the concept of *Sādhāraṇikaraṇa* and the concept of generalisation of Aristotle, *Dvani* and sublimity etc. can be undertaken. If our future scholars would be ready of undertake pain and shoulder the responsibility to this line of research for the development of Alaṅkāraśāstra, many more new results will definitely come to light. I hope the application of the modern stylistics to Indian literary theories will also yield fruitful results.

VII. Preparation of Encyclopedic, Bibliographical and Dictionary types of Works

We feel the urgent need of Bibliographical and Dictionary type of works in the field of Alaṅkāraśāstra. In the line of the works like *Encyclopedia of Indian Philosophies* prepared by Karl H. Potter, *Encyclopedia of Vedānta* by Prof. Ramamurti Sarma, Bibliographical works providing all the information about the printed books in different languages, different editions of original texts and commentaries, translations of poetic works and research papers and articles published so far should be taken up. That will facilitate fresh researchers and the scholars to collect their research material conveniently. Similarly the Bibliography of Ph.D., M. Phil. and D. Litt. theses which have been so far prepared in Indian Universities and Abroad should be prepared to have a large exposure to the students.

We also feel the need of preparing the Dictionary type of works in the line of *Nyāyakośa* by Bhimacarya and Mīmāṁsākośa etc. In this direction Prof. Brahmamitra Avasthi has already made a commendable effort and has prepared the *Alaṅkārakośa*. Another work of this type is *Dictionary* of *Sanskrit Poetics*. Similarly, a dictionary of poetic blemishes and the like, should be undertaken. All those works will be useful as tools of research and will facilitate our endeavour of researching and generating knowledge.

VIII. Translation Works

Since the standard of Sanskrit education has fallen down and teaching of Sanskrit in most of the Indian Universities is made in non-Sanskrit mediums like English, Gujarati, Hindi etc., most of the research-students feel the need of the translation of the original Sanskrit poetic texts. Though translations of earlier poetic works are available still there is a need of translations of some difficult earlier poetic works and post-Jagannātha works. That phase of Sanskrit poetics is in a neglected state of research.

IX. Study of Minor Poetic Works

There are some minor poeticians whose important contribution has so far not been realised. To some extent, they are different from well-known poeticians in propounding their novel views. Their works have not come into light and they have been neglected. To my mind, proper justice should be given to them also. It is required to collect the information about all those minor poeticians and their contributions to the field of Sanskrit poetics. Their ideas and novel thoughts should be studied carefully and our researchers should try to evaluate their efforts also carefully.

X. Study of Individual Alaṅkāras

There is a very extensive field of study, open for young scholars i.e. about individual Alaṅkāras. The study of Svabhāvokti, Atiśayokti, Rūpaka, and Utprekṣā has been made. There are many Alaṅkāras whose history and development are to be traced from very early times upto Jagannātha's time or even later. In the course of study of each *Alaṅkāra*, one will have to enter whether one likes or not, into the academic controversies between Appayadīkṣita and Jagannātha. Later Writers like Pradhānavenkamātya (author of *Alaṅkāramaṇidarpaṇa* unpublished), take the side of Appayyadīkṣita to defend and others like Lakṣmaṇasūri (author of *Śāhabhūpālaṅkāra-* unpublished) take the side of Jagannātha. It would be an academic feast and an occassion to re-construct the history of each Alaṅkāra.

XI Development of Modern Literary Criticism

There is not only the need of studying the critical literature of our ancient poeticians but also the need of creating new literary criticism. It is very important and essential for the reason that our modern Sanskrit literature has been developed to a great extent. With the demands of time a lot of development of various types, has taken place in the field of modern creative literature e.g. the poems of modern times. If we apply the principles of our ancient literary criticism to evaluate modern poets, then, we can't get satisfactory results and all those works of our ancient critics may not be completely helpful to us. It is, therefore, necessary that our researchers should also think in that direction and should attempt to create a body of new literary criticism which has stopped almost from the period of Jagannātha.

XII Critical Evaluation of Modern Studies on Alaṅkāraśāstra

Now, it is high time that we should also look at the studies which have been conducted so far in the field of Alaṅkāraśāstra. Critical evaluation of all those works is quite necessary. It will help us in understanding our needs, problems and progress. Unless and until it is done, we can not fully realize the areas which need research priority and study and how could a real advancement in the field of knowledge be made. Instead of going on the old roads and aiming at the things already achieved, our researchers should have new goals in mind and new ways to achieve them with new freshness.

15

KRISHNAMURTI : A PHILOSOPHICAL STUDY

Bijayananda Kar

Jiddu Krishnamurti (1895-1986) has been one of the most notable thinkers of our time. He has developed his thought on the basis of his long association with the great theosophist : Annie Besant. Of course, it is worth-noting that Krishnamurti has later on elaborated his thought on an independent original setting and his specific suggestion for deconditioning mind has attracted the attention of the mass. Throughout his speeches and writings, he has presented a critical attitude concerning intellectual enterprise and, in that way, he has even expressed his indifferent attitude towards philosophical reflection based on some rigoristic form of intellectualism or rationalism.

But, despite his general apathy towards philosophic enterprise, his point of view does indicate a philosophic stand which requires serious consideration as well as appraisal. With that end in view, here it is proposed to have a philosophical study of Krishnamurti's point of view.

Unlike the conventional philosophers, he never has presented his views in usual systematic form. As a matter of fact, one notices in his writings and speeches, the cluster of thoughts. In that way, it is no doubt, difficult, if not impossible, in making a proper estimation of his point of view. It seems, he has all through advocated for freedom from all sorts of fears and apprehensions. In this context, he has referred to be free from religious dogmas, desire for attaining salvation, aspiration for acquiring spiritual excellence. In his own words, "my only concern is to set man absolutely, unconditionally free". This reveals that freedom is the core point of focus in Krishnamurti's thought. And, freedom, according to him, centres around man of course. By freedom, he means something intrinsically concerning man alone. Man, as an individual, has the natural urge to be free from all sorts of external bonds of society, culture and tradition. However, thereby it is not suggestive that Krishnamurti's concept of freedom is purely egoistic. It does not suffer from individual idiosyncrasies, whimsicalities and oddities. It, on the other hand, seeks to emphasise on the control of external imposition and pressure on the free flow of human thought. This sense of freedom is not the mark of a visionary ideal but, to Krishnamurti, it is real and is felt by the person who sincerely pursues it.

Awareness of this concept of freedom is possible when man, as an individual, is to look within himself and that is why there is such emphasis on understanding of one's own self. However, before Krishnamurti, one comes across number of thinkers both from East and West emphasising on self-knowledge. "Know thyself' or "*Ātmānam viddhi*" are the important instances in this regard. But the significance of Krishnamurti's point of view is that he has advocated for the understanding of one's own self not as something distinct or transcendent from nature and the environment. Person being in the world is not denied but is conceded as real. Any transcendental notion of men has no place in his thought-construction. In this sense, there is the advocacy of integration and harmony between man's being and the world- process. This means, one has not to look for anything beyond but to realise the sense of proper freedom only amidst the worldly setting. Ordinarily awareness of this sense of freedom is not possible on account of being tied with the false sense of differences and the relations being caused thereby. All such false notions are due to the functioning of mind which cannot operate, according to Krishnamurti, unless there is pre-acceptance of differences and relations. Hence, his appeal is for *deconditioning of the mind*. It is, by way of such deconditioning or non-verbalisation, there is proper modification and man realises himself in the midst of natural setting. Man is never conceived as beyond nature.

Though Krishnamurti seems to have favoured an absolutistic conception of reality devoid of all relations he, nevertheless, has opted for a dynamic conception where there is scope for change and transformation. Man, in order to realise his being, has to transform himself within the worldly set up. The present actuality is never denied. Rather, on the contrary, each and every moment is considered as unique in itself and man, in his own person, is to face the challanges of life with freshness and novelty. Krishnamurti appeals for not brooding over the past. For, it is the sense of past which psychologically binds man with tension and sufferings and thus it stands as a definite hindrance for freedom and release. So also the desire to control the future amounts to the growth of tension and, in that way, blocks the free flow of the sense of freedom. Hence, Krishnamurti is critical about memory of past as well as expectation about future. By emphasising on the uniqueness of each moment of experience, a novel sense of creativity is explored in the very being of human personality. It is conducive for living and this is not life-transcending or life-negating. To him, the freedom of man consists in an intrinsic sense of creativity.

Another important point which is focussed in Krishnamurti's point of view is what he terms as "freedom from the known". It is the craving for knowledge which according to him, is based on desire and aspiration. It is the desire to know more and more that gives rise to selecting some instead of other, choosing some and leaving the rest. But, once there is scope for selection and choice, there is the beginning of aspirations and ambitions. And, as such, there is no peace but worries and anxieties. Proper sense of freedom is there where there is no scope for choice or selection. Even the desire for attaining freedom is critically viewed in this context. Because that state of mind is also rooted in a state of bondage consisting of worries and expectations. In this context, Krishnamurti's suggestion is for making oneself free from the shackles of knowledge. Freedom is a natural state of mind, a point of awareness, an affair of feeling. Hence he opts for a state of choiceless awareness which, transcends 'the desire for freedom'. To him, the very desire and effort to be free is an obstacle to freedom. Freedom is, in this sense, possible not by hankering after it. It is not one ideal to be achieved. It is already there, only it is to be realised. Here, one is reminded of a move undertaken by Bertrand Russell in his well known work, *In Praise of Idleness* where the celebrated author casts doubts with regard to the rapid movement of knowledge and prefers the state of idleness.

It is, of course, the deconditioning of mind which seems to be the core point of emphasis throughout the view held by Krishnamurti. This deconditioning is possible by making oneself free from knowing, believing and remembering the past. He also appeals for not being tied with any set of culture and tradition. There must be the spirit of openness to move freely not being confined to any set of ideas and beliefs, however deep-rooted those are in any traditional or cultural set up. This attitude of questioning everything in an open mind is quite significant. For, it reveals an important element of philosophic temper in his thinking. Philosophers, down the ages, are identified as those thinkers who are distinguished also in being critical and thereby questioning and challenging anything whatsoever, despite its long standing traditional basis.

This is likely to suggest that man, being critical about tradition, culture, and anything that arrests his unique sense of freedom, remains in a state of solitude, being confined to himself. If this be the account of free man, then man is viewed in terms of himself alone, completely being delinked from any mark of sociality. In fact Krishnamurti himself admits that such an account of freedom implies being fully alone. In this sense complete solitude is taken as the necessary condition of freedom. It is by means of getting oneself out from what he terms as superficial consciousness and grasping the deeper consciousness, one is led for the awareness of freedom. However, Krishnamurti's prescription for solitude of man, though apparently sounds as somewhat subjectivistic, transcends, as a matter of fact, privacy as well as publicity. He does not entertain any authority either of others or of one's own self, so far as awareness of freedom is concerned. It not only means freedom from the Known, it also stands for freedom from all kinds of dependence or slavery. Any sense of authoritarianism is not approved in this context. It is the awareness of oneself in the worldly set up in an extra- ordinary sense of openness that is based on the coolness of brain and composed state of intellect. Here the mind is restored to its original state of calmness, free from all sorts of conditioning which cause worries and tensions. This can be attained through pure silence, that transcends thought and language.

From all these discussions, it appears that Krishnamurti is deeply concerned about human freedom. His sincerity of approach need not be questioned. That he has carefully tried to avoid any subjective, authoritarian and theologically superimposed account of freedom is, perhaps, undeniable. That he takes up the issue of freedom in an open fresh mind without having any present theorisation may be undisputed. But, all the same, his final point of taking recourse to silence and non-verbalisation seems to close the door for any meaningful comprehension. It seems to carry all the limitations of any mystical rendering on account of taking such a step at last.

16

THE TERM KĀRAKA AND ITS PRINCIPAL AND SUBORDINATE NATURE

Achyutananda Dash

Professor B.K. Matilal, a fore-most thinker and an authoritative writer on Indian Philosophical works, remarks on the *kāraka* theory in an article "Indian Philosophy of Language" published posthumously.

> The concept of *kāraka* was presumably clear to the native language user as it was to Pāṇini. But it is almost impossible to define it or to find a *lakṣaṇa,* i.e. a uniquely distinguishing feature that would belong to all and only the six well-known *kārakas*. Various alternative definitions that have been suggested, in order to try to capture this intuition, but they fail to do so completely".[1]

A serious attention is to be paid to this remark. It opens the scope of asking a question: whether the *kāraka* is definable or not, in one hand and it challenges the long standing traditions on the other, which takes for granted that the term *kāraka* is a derivative and self-explanatory term, being defined variously in various schools of Indian Philosophy. We have tried to give a synthetic definition of *kāraka* in the next chapter giving a thorough survey of the traditional definitions with a classified approach to its different aspects, which is based on a historical perspective.[2] But, Matilal's remarks, even if not taken in isolation, seems to be challenging the traditional methodology in defining the *kāraka,* which is not true. On the contrary, in the same paper and elsewhere, Matilal tries to define the *kāraka* traditionally following the guidelines given by Bhavānanda, a Navya Naiyāyika of 15th/16th century A.D. But at the end, Matilal's remark on the *kāraka* definition, obviously shows his dissatisfaction (*asvārasyam*) very clearly. We find a similar *asvārasyam* in the statements of Bhoja Deva, a versatile author and ruler of the Central India in 10th / 11th century A.D., in his *magnum opus* work *Śṛṅgāraprakāśa*.

Kārakaśabdaścāyam avyutpannaḥ kriyānimittavacano lokatas siddhaḥ.[3] i.e. the term *kāraka* is underivative, used in the sense of the efficient cause of the action based on popular use. At the same time, Bhoja Deva,of course, defines the *kāraka* as: (1) *svaparāśritakriyābhinivṛttihetus śaktimad dravyam, yad dravyam kārakam ity ācakṣate* or (2) *karotīti kārakaśabdena śaktimad dravyam ucyate* i.e. The first definition means - it is the entity being called *kāraka* which is possessive of the potentialities, conductive to the efficient cause of the action, and the second definition means - the potential entity is called *kāraka* since, it accomplishes the main action. Here, Bhoja Deva's first definition is based on Bhartṛhari's VP. III. 7.1[5] and the second definition is based on the etymological definition of the term as given by Patañjali, the author of *Mahābhāṣya.*[6]

Therefore, it is very clear from the above discussion that there is some controversies on the term *kāraka* itself as (1) whether it is derivative or non-derivative, or rather is it an irregular term ? (2) whether it is definable or not ? If not, to what extent ? Thus, here we are interested to focus on two aspects of the term *kāraka* : (1) the controversy on the etymology of the term *kāraka* and its contribution to the definition. (2) the two-fold classification of *kāraka* viz. *mukhya* (principal) and *gauṇa* (subordinate) *kāraka.*

Kāraka - the term, certainly, is derivative. It is derived from the verbal base *kṛ* - "to do" with the primary suffix *Ṇvul* (p. 3.1.133 and p. 7.1.1) in the sense of *kartā* (doer). Whole tradition, starting from Patañjali, derives the term *kāraka* in the same manner and presumably satisfied with it. Patañjali, goes to the extent that, the reason behind designating a long-term (*mahatī saṃjñā*) is to make the term significant (*anvarthasamjñā*).[7] But, if some one goes very strictly with the etymology, it will mean only the "agent" (*kartā*) for the reason stated above. In other words, the term *kāraka,* therefore, will mean a "doer" i.e. it would be synonymous with the agent, (*kartṛ-kāraka*) only. In that case the problem will be :

(1) Either there will be only one *kāraka* viz. *kartṛ- kāraka* alone

(2) If the term *kāraka* is applicable to all other *kārakas* then, they might be called as :

* *karma-kartṛ* for *karma-kāraka*

* *karaṇa-kartṛ* for *karana-kāraka*

* *sampradāna-kartṛ* for *sampradāna-kāraka*

* *apādāna-kartṛ* for *apādāṇa-kāraka*
* *adhikaraṇa-kartṛ* for *adhikaraṇa-kāraka*.

And if these terms are accepted to be correct, then there will be a logical fallacy called *kāraka-sāṁkarya*, which is not at all desirable. Hence, the tradition never uses this term strictly in its etymological sense, but rather in a loose sense referring to the whole *kāraka* class. In other words, *kāraka* is a general term represents the *kāraka-cakra* and *kartṛ* etc., are specific terms refer to the individual *kārakas* depending upon their particular role played by them in the accomplishment of the main action. Therefore, *kāraka*, the general term and *kartṛ* etc., the particular terms have a *vyāpya-vyāpaka-bhāva* relationship amongst themselves and thus, *kāraka-sāṁkarya prasaṅga* would not arise.

It seems, the problem form Bhoja was : How to justify and identify this distinction of *kāraka*, i.e. one in general sense and the other in particular sense. This cannot be done on the basis of the etymology. Hence, he says : *kārakaśabdaś cāyam avyutpannaḥ* so that it can refer to its general sense.

The second part of the problem is that each and every *kāraka* would have been treated as *kartṛ-kāraka* only. To reply this, Bhoja quotes the following *kārikās* of Bhartṛhari:

niṣpattimātre kartṛtvam sarvatraivāsti kārakaḥ/
vyāpārabhedāpekṣāyām karaṇāditvasaṁbhavaḥ//
putrasya janmani yathā pitroḥ kartṛtvamucyate/
ayamasyāmiyam tvasmāditi bhedo vivakṣayā//

With reference to merely bringing about an action, each and every *kāraka* could be (treated as) the agent, but due to (their) distinct function, the instrumentality etc., are justified. For instance, as far as the birth of the offspring is concerned, both the parents are said to be the agents. But according to the desire of the speaker, the distinction could be - he (the father causes the birth of the offspring) in her, and she (in the same manner) from him.

There is a long discussion on this issue in Patañjali's *Mahābhāṣya*.[9] Obviously, Bhartṛhari's view is based on this portion of Mbh. But, the interesting point is, at the end of the whole discussion, Patañjali has suggested a new sense of the term *kāraka* meaning *kriyā*.[10] This, definitely is a suggestion astray, which is not taken seriously in the tradition. But, it certainly shows his dissatisfaction in the whole argument on p. 1.4.23. Therefore, he thinks, let the term *kāraka* mean *kriyā*. Possibly, Patañjali, takes the term *kāraka* very much in its etymological sense, and then, *kāraka* would mean *kriyā* only if the suffix *ṇvul* is used in the sense of *bhāva*. But we do not find any such instance where, the suffix *ṇvul* is used in the sense of *bhāva*. Therefore, we are at a loss to justify Patañjali in this matter. Kaiyaṭa and Nāgeśa extend their full support to Patañjali with a pinch of salt.[11] Prof. Joshi thinks that the interpretation given by Kaiyaṭa and Nāgeśa is not correct.[12] According to Joshi, Patañjali's effort is to give a textual justification of Paṇini's *sūtras* p. 1.4.23 in the sense of *kriyānvayitva* i.e., connection with an action. Joshi's point is remarkable and it refers to the semantico-syntactic aspect of the *kāraka*, which takes altogether a different dimension, free from the etymological aspect of the term. But, this interpretation again, does not solve the problem as far as the co-referential and complementary nature of the term *kāraka* to be used along with the other *kārakas* viz. *karma-kāraka, kāraṇa- kāraka* etc., is concerned. Moreover, Prof. Joshi's interpretation, though correct logically and ontologically, still, it does not suit the context in Patañjali's *Mahābhāṣya*.

It is therefore, to solve the aforesaid problem, we can find some justification in Bhoja's interpretation of the term, referreing to the *kāraka*-class in its general sense in one hand and giving the etymological definition on the other.

In this connection only, Bhavānanda's two-fold classification of *kāraka* in primary (*mukhya*) and secondary (*gauṇa*) sense of the term is interesting. Moreover, Bhavānanda gives two distinct definitions of these *mukhya* and *gauṇa kārakas*, which fundamentally takes a diverse direction from that of the old School of Nyāya. Let us examine the difference of interpretations on one and the same concept in the old and Neo-schools of Nyāya and try to trace the cause of the diversion.

Bhavānanda defines *kāraka* as : *vibhaktyarthadvārā kriyānvayitvam mukhya-bhākta-sādhāraṇam kārakatvam, kriya'nimittatvasahitam mukhyam iti,*[13] being a *kāraka*, common to (both) the primary as well as the secondary sense (of *kāraka*) is that; which is syntactically related to the *kriyā* (the import of the verbal base) through the import of the case ending. The primary *kāraka* is (defined as) that, which is (also) the efficient cause of the action.

According to Bhavānanda, *kāraka* should be seen and defined from two conceptual point of views. One, he calls, *mukhya- kāraka* and the other *gauṇa kāraka*. As per his definition, *kāraka* is that, which is significant as far as the semantic role of the *kāraka* is concerned and at the same time, it governs the syntactic role, only through the import of the case-endings, being indifferent to its semantic significance. The semantic significance of *kāraka* refers to only its role that it plays in accordance with the accomplishment of the main action as the efficient cause. Therefore, we can reconstrue the definition of *mukhya kāraka* and *gauṇa kāraka* respectively as : *kriyānimittatve sati vibhaktyarthadvārā mukhyakārakatvam* :

Kriyāyā animittatve sati vibhaktyarthadvārā kriyānvayitvam gauṇa kārakatvam.

The qualifying term viz. *kriyānimittatva,* in these two definitions causes the difference by way of its presence and absence respectively in *mukhya* and *gauṇa kāraka*. The concept of *kriyānimittatva* comes from the very etymology of the term *kāraka,* i.e. *karotīti kārakam iti*. The verb *karoti* means *kriyām janayati/niṣpādayati,* i.e. which accomplishes the main action according to the school of grammar.[14]

Yatna/kṛti is said to be in the *ātman* and therefore, the sense of *karoti* is primarily applicable to the animate beings only. Hence, the Naiyāyikas accept that the *kriyānimittatva* concept can suitably be applicable only to a *sacetana padārtha* but never to an *acetana padārtha* in its primary sense. In other words, in case, the verb *karoti* is used governing the agency of an inanimate entity, then it should be taken as a secondary (*gauṇa/bhākta*) usage. This is the fundamental reason for the Naiyāyikas to accept the *kāraka* being two-fold viz. *mukhya* and *gauṇa* and the *mukhya* is *kriyānimitta* as well as *kriyānvayi;* but the *gauṇa* is only *kriyānvayi*.

On the contrary, according to the school of grammar the verbal base *kṛ* (means *vyāpāra* action) only and the action as such, could be seen in any entity, irrespective of it being animate or inanimate. They say, there is no reason what so ever, to accept the verbal base *kṛ* mean *yatna/kṛti,* which is *ātmaniṣṭha*. Therefore, the two-fold classification as has been stated above, not deemed to be necessary in the school of grammar. Thus, in the sentences like :

(1) *Devadattaḥ pacati,* 'Devadatta cooks'

(2) *Yajñadattaḥ gacchati,* 'Yajñadatta goes'

(3) *Sthālī pacati,* 'The cauldron cooks'

(4) *Ratho gacchati,* 'The cart goes'

All the nominatives viz., *Devadatta* in (1), *Yajñadatta* in (2), *sthālī* in (3) and *ratha* in (4) are treated as agents '(*kartāraḥ*) equally as far as the accomplishment of their action is concerned. But according to the school of Nyāya, Devadatta and Yajñadatta in (1) & (2) are primary agents and *sthālī* and *ratha* are secondary agents, since they are inanimate entities.

However, the old school of Nyāya, especially Uddyotakara and Vācaspati Miśra, though accept the two-fold classification of the *kāraka* as *mukhya* and *gauṇa,* still, they do so entirely on a different ground. According to Uddyotakara and Vācaspati Miśra, the essential nature of *kāraka* is *śakti,*[15] which has been strictly denied in the Navya Nyāya, even by Jayanta Bhaṭṭa,[16] who belongs to the old school. Vārttikakāra defines the *mukhya kāraka* as the entity, possessive of the potency, which becomes conductive to the accomplishment of the main action and at the same time, of it (i.e. the entity) is logically and ontologically related to the action (*kriyā*).[17] However, why the entity is not related to the *kriyā* logically or ontologically, but it is possessive of the eternal potency, then it is secondary *kāraka.*[18] Vācaspati Miśra, commenting upon Uddyotakara, says: *śakti-kriyāsambandhayor kārakaśadyo mukhya śaktimātre tu gauṇa iti,* i.e. whenever the term *kāraka* is used in accordance with potency and the syntactico-semantic relation with action, then it (*kāraka*) : otherwise, when the term *kāraka* issued only with reference to the potency, then it is treated as *gauṇa kāraka.*

It seems that the latter Naiyāyikas have not taken, into account the above said interpretation of *mukhya* and *gauṇa kāraka* by Uddyotakara and Vācaspati Miśra, though this theory is very much relevant in the school of grammar and hotly debated by the Navya Naiyāyikas. This is presumbly because of the strict denial of *śakti padārtha* in the school of Navya Nyāya.

Bhavānanda's concept of *mukhya* and *gauṇa kāraka* is quite different from that of Uddyotakara and Vācaspati Miśra. But as we have already mentioned above that the grammarians do not agree with either of the views. For them, no such *gauṇa-mukhya* gradation is applicable to the *kāraka* theory, where the *śabda* is supposed to speak of the sense. Thus, the often quoted statement of Patañjali viz. *śabdapramāṇakā vayam, yacchabda āha tad asmākam pramāṇam* is quite relevant here. Bhartṛhari says :

dharmair abhyuditais śabde niyamo na tu vastuni/
kartur dharmavivakṣāyām śabdāt kartā pratīyate//[19]

This means, as and when the intrinsic properties are expressed, the syntactic rules (governing and binding as per the verb in the sentence is concerned) are applicable to the words only but not to the import of the words, when there is an intention of the speaker approves to present any entity as the agent of the action, the same is recognised as agent by the expression itself. Helārāja, commenting upon this *kāraka* says : *śabdena yasyaite dharmāḥ pratīyayante sa kartā boddhavyaḥ, na tu vastuviṣayatavād dharmāṇām eṣām sambhavo 'nvasaṇīyaḥ yenācetanaviṣaya agnir dahati, edhāḥ pacanti, sthālī pacati, ity ādau, kūlam patati, nadī vahati, ity ādau ca kartṛtvam na syāt.*[20]

Helārāja just translates the views of Bhartṛhari. But his examples are interesting. These usages show that there are some *kriyās* though accomplished by the inanimate beings, still there is a prompter, presumably an animate being behind the activities, who sets the *kārakas* in order to be accomplished by some natural phenomena, whose agency can not satisfactorily be defined as *mukhya* or *gauṇa kārakas*. This issue, therefore, may further be extended to highly philosophical discourse like what should be the criteria of identifying the animacy and inanimacy of phenomenal and logical entities ? Even if some phenomenal and logical entities are taken for granted to be animate beings, do they have the similar *yatna / kṛti* as we find in well developed animals like that of human beings ? Moreover, there are some activities accomplished by the animate and inanimate beings equally without having a *yatna/kṛti*. In that case, how to justify the *mukhya kārakatva* or *gauṇa kārakatva* of the entity ? Let us examine some usages :

(5) *Caitro gacchati,*	'Chitra goes'
(6) *Ratho gacchati,*	'The cart goes'
(7) *Kālo gacchati,*	'Time goes on'
(8) *Mano gacchati,*	'Mind goes'
(9) *Dharmo gacchati,*	'The dharma goes'
(10) *phalam patati*	'The fruit falls'

(11) *bālaḥ patati* 'The child falls'

(12) *kūlam patati,* 'The bank (of the river) falls'

(13) *ulkā patati,* 'The meteor falls'

(14) *sarvataḥ vipadaḥ patanti,* 'Calamities falling from all sides'.

The *kriyā, 'gacchati'* governs the agency of the nominative in 5 - 9 usages and the *kriyā 'patati'* in 10-14. According to Bhavānanda's definition of *mukhya* and *gauṇa kāraka,* the usages viz. (5) and (11) would be treated as *mukhya kāraka*. Rest of the usages would be treated as *gauṇa kārakas*. But the question is, does the *bālaḥ*, the child' in (11) have a *yatna/kṛti* (volitional effort) to fall ? On the contrary the child's whole effort is to stand up and not to fall. Then how can it be treated as *mukhya kāraka* (*kariyā* in present case)? In fact, no agent governed by the *patati kriyā,* unless otherwise intended, could be *mukhya kāraka*. So also, let us take the usage (7) *kālo gacchati* 'Time goes''. What is this *kāla*? How does it go? Is it an animate or inanimate entity ? To answer all these questions, it may take a long and inconclusive philosophical discource and finally we may not be able to identify or justify whether this expression is an example of *mukhya kāraka* or *gauṇa kāraka*. The same argument may suitably be applicable to the usages (8) and (9). Therefore, to our judgement, the *kāraka* classification like *mukhya* and *gauṇa* is not deemed to be necessary as far as the *kāraka* theory is concerned. It is thus, the Grammarian's theory on linguistic issues in general and *kāraka* theory in particular and more logical and just.

In this context, another point may be noted that the old school of Nyāya was quite at home with the linguistic issues and they had no dogmatic attitude towards language philosophy. We have seen here only that Uddyotakara and Vācaspati Miśra, both openly accept the *śaktiḥ kārakam* theory of the grammarians which is not at all acceptable to the Navya Nyāya. This shows that in those days there was a give and take relationship amongst the Philosophical schools and they have an accomodative attitude on the theoretical issues. They differ, only when the fundamental concepts contradictory. This is necessary to uphold the distinct identity of each and every school of thought. But we, the students of Indian Philosophy, should cultivate a noble, harmonious and synthetic as well as distinguishing attitude like : *paramatam anumatam bhavati asati bādhake* to study the Philosophical works.

REFERENCES

1. Motilal, B.K., *"Indian philosophy of Language"*, (a tri-lingual volume published in German, English and French), Vol. I, ed. by Marcelo Dascal et al. Walter de Gruyter, Berlin, New York, 1992 p. 87.
2. Dash, Achyutananda, *"Kāraka Definition-Revistited"*. ed. by R.V. Tripathi et al., Pratibha Prakashan, Delhi, 1993, pp. 111-135.
3. *Ibid*. p. 145.
4. *Ibid*., p. 145.
5. *Svāsraye samavetānām tadvad evāśrayāntare/ kriyāṇām abhinispatau sāmarthyam sādhanam vihuḥ//* (v.p. III. 7.1).
6. Karotīti Kārakam iti - Māhābhāṣya of Patañjali (Mbh.), Vol. I. ed. F. Kielhorn. Fouth edn. BORI, Poona, 1985, p. 324.
7. *Kāraka iti mahatī samjñā Kriyate, Saṁjñā ca nāmayato na laghiyaḥ kuta etat? laghvartham hi samjñākaraṇam, tatra mahatyāḥ samjñāyā karaṇa etat prayojanam anvarthasamjñā yathā vijñāyeta. Mbh ibid.* Vol. I. p. 324.
8. VP. III. 7.18-19.
9. See Mbh. on *Vārttika* 6 to 15 on p. 1.4.23, Vol. I ibid. pp. 324- 326.
10. *Athavā yāvad brūyād kriyāyām iti tāvat kāraka iti*, Mbh. Ibid. p. 326.
11. *Kriyātra sūtre kāraka śabdenocyate. Sā hi kartarādini visiṣṭa vyadeśayuktāni karoti, Pradīpa* on p. 1.4.23; and *"nanu kārakā-śabdāloke kriyāpratitir na dṛṣṭā ity āta - sūtra it*, Nāgeśa, *Uddyota* on *Pradîpa*.
12. Joshi, S.D., and Rodbergen. J.A.F., 1975, (1.4.55), University of Poona, Poona. p. 50.
13. *Kārakacakram*, by Bhavānanda Siddhāntavāgīśa, with com. *Mādhavī* by Madhava Tarkālaṅkāra and Notes *Pradīpa* by Sītāśaraṇa Tripathi, ed. with Intro. etc. by Brahma Shankara Shastri, Haridas Sanskrit Series, 154, CSSO, Varanasi, 1942. p. 5.
14. *Kṛtākṛtavibhāgādinā kṛdhātor yatnārthakatve niścite āśrayārthakatṛjanta kṛdhātuvyutpannakartṛapadasya yatnāśrayārthadodhakatvācca, aretane katṛpadaprayogo Gauṇah*, of Bhavananda, with Comm. *Mādhavī and Pradīa, Ibid*. p. 15.
15. *Yadi kriyāsambhandhanimittakaḥ kārakaśabdaprayogaḥ pacaty eve pācaksabdaḥ pravarteta nāpākṣīt pācakaḥ, pakṣati pācaka iti? na, śaktestrikālāvasthānāt - pakṣatīti kāpunar iyam śaktiḥ kriy'kartṛvyatiriktaḥ kartṛdharmaḥ. Sāmarthyam upāyaparijñānam ca kriyāsambandhena vyavatiṣṭate.* Uddyotakara *on* 2.1.16.
16. *See Nyāyamañjarī by Jayanta Bhaṭṭa CSSO*, Varanasi, p. 17.
17. *Yadopāyavijñānasāmarthyakriyāsambandhas tata mukhyataḥ Kārakaśabdaḥ* pravartate, Nyāyavśrttika (NV.) Nyāyadarśanam, ed. by Taranath Tarkatirtha, Munsiram Manoharlal, New Delhi, p. 440.
18. *Yadā tu kriyāsambandham antarenopāyaparij«ānas-āmarthyamātro pādānenyatamavikalyāt pāckaśabdaḥ pravartate tadopacāraḥ NV. Ibid.*, p. 440.
19. V.P. III. 7.103.
20. Helārāja on V.P. III. 7. 103. DCPRI, Poona edn. p. 313.

17

HOLIDAYS (ANADHYĀYAS) IN ANCIENT EDUCATIONAL SYSTEM

S.G. Moghe

MM. Dr. P.V. Kane has given a very exhaustive treatment to this topic in his monumental work, *History of Dharmaśāstra*, Vol. II/I. pp. 292-402, by consulting Dharma-Sūtras and the Smṛtis and the commentaries on the same. He has also made incidental references to the digest works like the *Smṛticandrikā* and the commentary of Aparārka on the *Yājñavalkya-Smṛti*, which is also of the nature of a digest.

The expression *Anadhyāya* used in the context of the Dharmaśāstra literature is generally translated as 'holiday, or interruption'. I have preferred to translate here as a 'holiday'.

If one seriously considers the discussion introduced by Dr. Kane, one would form the impression that in ancient India, education was primarily concerned with the recitation of the Vedic *mantras*. Hence the holidays were introduced in view of the different situations. For the purpose of a holiday, however, the different grounds such as place, time, smell of bad things, fright, conveyances, musical instruments, natural phenomena, festivals, natural calamities, death of the important persons, the shades of the particularly mentioned trees are considered by the writers on Dharmaśāstra.

It may be mentioned here confidently that Dr. Kane has not consulted the sources of the *Gṛhyasūtra* literature, some digest works and the astrological works for the purpose of holidays. Hence by consulting the sources unexplored by Dr. Kane, for the discussion, I would like to bring the discussion nearer to the peak of perfection. In this paper, therefore, the readers will find that matter which has escaped the eagle eye of MM. Dr. Kane or the matter for which he could not give more serious thoughts.

I would like to distribute the matter under three heads - digest works, *Gṛhyasūtra* works and Astrological works.

Before beginning with the digest matter, I first mention one important place of the *Gautama Dharma-Sūtra* (GDS) 16.34. This *Sūtra* provides that there should be no study particularly in the *Manuṣya-yajña* and the gathering of friends and the lunch of the brahmins. Here it should be noted that the expression *'Manuṣya-yajña'* in the above *sūtra*, is rendered by Maśkari[1] as *mitramelaka.* i.e. the gathering of friends.

Incidentally, the importance of the *Gṛhyasūtra* literature in this context is not ignored by Maśkari who is chronologically later than Haradatta. In his comments on the *Gautama-Dharma- Sūtra* 16.50, Maśkari stresses[2] the views of the Gṛhyasūtrakāras and the word *ca* in the *sūtra* makes the inclusion of other religious creeds.

As regards the material scattered in the digest works, I draw the attention of the readers to the *Brahmacāri-kāṇḍa* of the *Kṛtyakalpataru* of Lakṣmīdhara. He quoted *Vaśiṣtha Dharma-Sūtra* 13.35 which states[3] that there should not be study at the fall of a mountain, sand, blood from the sky etc. Dr. Kane seems to be quite conscious[4] of this reference since he has mentioned only this exact place of the *Vaśiṣtha Dharma- Sūtra* in the course of his discussion, only in the bracket. This matter can be included in the portentous phenomena such as rain of blood and stones.

In the *Brahmacāri-Kāṇḍa* of the *Kṛtyakalpataru* p. 251, Lakṣmīdhara quotes the view of Baudhāyana.[5] (This is possibly a reference to the *Baudhāyana Śrautra-Sūtra,* since the passage relied upon by Lakṣmīdhara is not found in the extant *Baudhāyana Dharma-Sūtra* with the commentary of Govindaswāmī). The view of Baudhāyana is that there should be the holiday for one day on the death of a *deśapati, Śrotrīya* and *Ekatīrtha.* Here it is interesting to note that Lakṣmīdhara explains[6] *'deśapati'* as a soldier and refers to the Yājñavalkya who declares three days as holidays on the death of a king. Even Hārita shares this view of Yājñavalkya.

If, however, we consult the *Smṛticandrikā-Saṁskāra-Kāṇḍa* of Devaṇṇabhaṭṭa, we get additional matter on holidays. Devaṇṇabhaṭṭa in his *Smṛticandrikā Saṁskāra-Kāṇḍa* quotes a passage from the Purāṇa (without disclosing the source) to the effect[7] that one should observe holiday on *Trayodaśī, Saptamī* and the evening of *caturthī,* only if one is desirous of having sufficient growth in his intelligence. From this quotation, it is evident that the concept of holiday is connected with human intellectual progress and time element. This view has escaped the notices of Dr. Kane.

As regards the places to be avoided for the study of the Veda, Dr. Kane has referred to the *Yājñavalkya-Smṛti* I. 148- 151 in the *History of Dharmaśāstra* Vol. II/I p. 396. But he has not considered a reference to the quotation from the text of *Pracetas* quoted by Devaṇṇabhaṭṭa. The citation[8] from *Pracetas* simply means that there should be no study at a place where four roads meet, on the high way, on the street, in the garden and near the temple.

Dr. Kane has referred to the view of Yājñavalkya that there should be no study on the arrival of a distinguished visitor to the house of a person. Devaṇṇabhaṭṭa adds a very important view[9] of Yama that even if a distinguished guest permits, one should not start with the Vedic study.

Coming to the important digest of *Nirṇayasindhu* by Kamalākara-bhaṭṭa, one notices that he has laid stress on the *Gautama-Dharma-Sūtra*[10] XVI. 42 (which has escaped the eye of Kane) that there should be no study after a lunch in a festival. Here Maskari in his comments on the *Gautama Dharma- Sūtra* explains that *abhyudaya* has a reference to the all round prosperity and the festival refers[11] to the thread ceremony of a boy. This is certainly a different explanation of the words that have occured in the *Sūtras*.

If, however, we refer to another digest-work known as *Saṁskāra-kaustubha* of Anantadeva, we have a very important quotation. He quotes a passage[12] which means that when the animals or an ungrateful person passes between the two persons standing on the road, then he should observe a holiday completely. Here it should be noted only incidentally that a mention of an ungrateful person is treated as a sign for the holiday. This point is not at all touched by Dr. Kane. Hence this point deserves mention in this context. Here it may also be observed that for an ungrateful person, there is no expiation laid down by the Dharmaśāstra authors. Here this is further considered as a sign for a holiday, since such a person who is most ungrateful, has become the object of odium in ancient India.

In the *Saṁskārakaustubha* Anantadeva refers to the view of Gārga[13] who holds that the *dvitīyās* of four months (*Cāturmāsyās*) should be treated as holidays. Here he specifically points out that the *dvitīyās* of the months *Āṣāḍha, Kārtika* and *Phālguna*. These *dvitīyās* should be of the black fortnight. This view is further supported by quoting a stanza in this respect.

Now coming to the *Gṛhyasūtra* literature, we have the interesting material in the Pāraskara, Gobhila and *Sāṁkhāyana-Gṛhya-Sūtras*.

In the *Pāraskara-Gṛhyasūtra* II. 11.5, it is said that at the sight of a person charged with a crime, a *patīta* person and on the occasions of prosperity and wonderful events, there should be an occasional holiday. The expression *'Abhyudaya'* in the above *sūtra*, is taken by Harihara[15] as having a reference to the birth of a son and marriage. Viśvanātha agrees with Harihara on this point. Gadādhara, however, in his comments takes the wonderful events[16] as having a reference to the magic play of a magician. It is worth noting that even the sight of a *patita* and a criminally charged person was disliked by the people.

In the *Pāraskara-Gṛhyaśūtra* II. 11.6, it is held that the particularly described behaviour of a *śiṣṭa* should be treated as a cause of holiday. The expression' *śiṣṭa* is rendered[17] as *śrotrīya* by both the commentators Harihara and Gadādhara. This view is also found expressed in the *Gobhila-Gṛhyaśūtra* III. 3.29. The *Saṁskārakaustubha* p. 567 states that when the *śiṣṭa* has come to the house, there should be no study at all.

There is an identical view expressed in the *Drāhyāyaṇa-Gṛhya- Sūtra* with the commentary of Rudraskāṇḍa III. 2.3 and *Mhādira Gṛhya Sūtra* III. 2.3031. These two *sūtras* maintain[18] that acording to the *Kaṭhas* and the *Kauthumas,* the study is forbidden when the rain has fallen and particularly as long as water remains in the ditches. Rudraskanda in his comments on the word *ca* states that by this word, we have to combine the views of other *smṛtis* and thereby one should understand other unrevealed occasions.

In the *Saṁkhyāyana-Gṛhya-Sūtra*[19] we have some peculiar views. In IV. 27.6, it is stated that the interruption in the Vedic recitation is to be followed on hearing what is forbidden. In IV. 7.34, it is further said that having climbed up a tree, one should observe a holiday. There should be further holidays on the occasions of shaving the hair and beard until the bath, as is clear from IV. 7.42. It further adds that there should be a holiday, on the occasion of oneself being rubbed. While bathing also this *anadhyāya* is recommended. When, however, one is having sexual intercourse, one should follow a holiday.

Coming to the Astrological literature, one would find that in the *Muhūtra-Mārtaṇḍa* with the commentary known as *Mārtaṇḍa- Vallabhā,* there is a stanza[20] quoted from the *Kūrmapurāṇa* that one should observe the holidays for three nights (i.e. three days) on the death of a person of equal lore, fellow- student and a teacher. It is further interesting to note that in the commentary *Pramitākṣarā* on the *Muhūrtacintāmaṇi* V. 164, a stanza[21] is quoted from the *Smṛti- Ratnāvalī* to the effect that so long as the sun rotates from the constellation Anurādhā upto further 16 constellations, there should be no recitation of the Vedic *mantras*. In the commentary known as *Pīyūṣa-dhārā* on the *Muhūrtacintāmaṇi* V. 54, a stanza is quoted from the *Jyotiḥsārasāgara* to the effect that according to Purāṇas there should be a holiday on the *dvitīyā* which falls at the end of the four months. It is worth noting here that these views of the works on *Muhūrta*-Astrology, are not at all considered by Dr. Kane.

In conclusion, it may be stated that the matter presented here in view of the sources unexplored by Dr. Kane is certainly interesting and adding to the matter which is already presented by him.

REFERENCES

1. मनुष्ययज्ञे मित्रमेलके । भोजने अनेकब्राह्मणभोजने ।
एतेष्वहोरात्रमनध्यायः । मस्करिon गौतमधर्मसूत्र ।16.34. p. 269, Mysore Edition, 1917.
2. प्रतिवेदं प्रतिशास्त्रं च याननध्यायान् गृह्यकाराःस्मरन्ति,चकाराद्धर्मान्तरेष्वपि,नाधीयीतेति सम्बन्धः । *Ibid*. p. 272.
3. दिङ्नागपवैतार्चाप्रपातिषूपलरुधिरपांसु वर्षेष्वाकमलकम् । कृत्यकल्पतरु, p. 257 Quoted in *वसिष्ठ सूत्र* 13.35.
4. P.V. Kane - *धर्मसूत्र,* Vol. II/I p. 399 B.O.R.I. Edition. 1974.
5. देशपति श्रौतियैकर्तार्थप्रायेणष्वहोरात्रमनध्यायः । बोधायनI 21.6 is quoted in कृत्यकल्पतरु-ब्रह्मचारिकाण्ड p. 251, Baroda Edition, 1948.
6. देशपतिःसैनिकादिः । *Ibid* p. 251.
7. मेधाकाम्यत्रयोदश्यां सप्तम्यां च विशेषतः ।
चतुर्थ्यां च प्रदोषेषु न स्मरेन्न च कीर्तयत् ॥
स्मृतिचंद्रिका-संस्कारकाण्ड, p. 154, Mysore Edition, 1914.
8. *Ibid*. p. 162.
9. *Ibid*., p. 164.
10. 16.43 p. 271 p. 276

11. *Ibid.*, p. 271.
12. गजसारससिंहव्याघ्रमहापातकिकृतघ्नादेरब्दम् । संस्कार-कौस्तुभः ,p. 568 with Marathi Translation by V.N. Upadhyaya, Śāstri, Baroda, 1914.
13. शुचावूर्जे तपस्ये च या द्वितीया विधुक्षये ।
    चातुर्मास्याद्वितीयास्ताः प्रवदन्ति मनीषिण इति ।*Ibid* p. 569.
14. धावतोऽभिशस्तपतितदर्शनाश्चर्याभ्युदयेषु च तत्कालम् । पारस्कर-गृह्यसूत्र,p. 279.
15. अभ्युदयः पुत्रजन्मविवाहादिः । हरिहर on पा.गृ.सू. p. 281.
16. आश्चर्यमद्भुतमिन्द्रजालादि ।गदाधर on पा.गृ.सू. p. 281.
17. शिष्टस्य श्रोत्रियस्य । गदाधर p. 283., Also हरिहर, p. 283
18. कार्ष्वं तु कठकौथुमाः । श्वादिरगृह्यसूत्र III 2.31 p. 112 (Published by Thakar Udaya Narayan Singh, Mozaffarpur, 1934) द्राह्मायण गृह्ययूत्र III 2.31 p. 112.
19. Sacred Books of the East Series -Vol XXIX. सांख्यायन-गृह्यसूत्र, Eng. Translation, Motilal Banarasidass, 1967 pp. 115-118.
20. रामानविद्ये तु मृते तथा सब्रह्मचारिणे ।
    आचार्ये संस्थिते चापि त्रिरात्रं क्षपणं स्मृतम् ॥ मार्तण्डवल्लभा Published by Gondhakkar, Bombay, saka 1816, p. 137.
21. Nirnaya Sagar press, Bombay 1928. p. 162.

18

ON THE MYTH (TS. 2.5.1) NARRATING THE ORIGIN OF MENSTRUATION

Nirmala Kulkarni

Introduction

Menstruation - a stage of crisis in the life cycle of a woman - receives much attention in almost all cultures. Today, because of the advancement in the understanding of physiology a few people render it as a typical bodily function of a mammal female. However, a mass of people cannot discard the cultural impressions cast for centuries. Though the physiological phenomenon is universal, the cultural implications differ and accordingly ritual details and taboos show variations. Present paper aims at getting some ideas of Vedic people regarding menstruation which are depicted in a myth of the *Taittirīya Saṁhitā* (TS 1.5.1).[1] It provides us a folk answer to the question why do women menstruate. A list of taboos is also appended to the myth. For the present discussion, however, I have confined myself just to the narration part. The discussion is arranged in the following manner :

1. English rendering of the myth
2. Versions of the myth
3. Observations
4. Conclusion

English Rendering of the Myth :

The myth under discussion occurs in the TS 2.5.1. It is also referred to in many Sanskrit works. As an appendix many prohibitory rules are cited in the myth which are also blotted down in later Sanskrit works. The following is the English rendering of the myth.

Viśvarūpa, son of Tvaṣṭṛ and nephew of the *Asuras*, was the priest of

Gods. He had three heads, one to drink *soma*, another to drink liquor and third to eat food. Openly he ensured portions of sacrificial oblations to the Gods; but secretly promised them to *Asuras*. When Indra came to know such deceipt, he got angry. "This is how my sovereignty is handed over to others', he exclaimed. With his thunderbolt he cut the three heads of Viśvarūpa. The *Somapāna* head turned into *Kapiñjala* (a hazzel cock, an omnious bird), *Surāpāna* into *Kalaviṅka* (a sparrow) and *Annadāna* into *Tittirī*, a pantidge. But since Indra had slaughtered a Brahmin, he had to bear Brahmanicide,[2] i.e. a sin caused by killing a *Brāhmaṇa*. He held it in his palms for over a year. All creatures blamed him and called him '*Brahmahan*'. Thereafter, he approached the Earth and appealed her to accept one-third portion of the sin. Accepting Indra's appeal she asked for a boon. As per her wish Indra gave her a boon "Digging will not cause any damage to you. In a year that portion will be refilled". Earth accepted the desired portion of the sin which turned into a barren land. Therefore, any *Āhitāgni* should not stay on such a land. Because it has got the colour of Brahminicide.

Then Indra approached plants and appealed them to accept one-third portion of the sin. Plants also asked for a boon. He assured, "even after trimming you will grow again". Plants accepted the sin and it turned into the sap. Therefore, one should not eat gum or sap either reddish or any colour which oozes from plants after cutting.

Thereafter he approached a concourse of women and also appealed them to accept the remaining portion of the sin. They asked for two boons. (i) Because of the accepted portion of the sin we should get progeny, (ii) till the birth of the child we should be able to unite with our partners. The sin of *Brahmahatyā* accepted by women turned into menstrual flow. Therefore one should not talk to her and food prepared by her should be avoided. Because she has fastened the colour of *Brahmahatyā* to her body.

Versions of the Myth

The *Rāmāyaṇa*, the *Skandapurāṇa*, the *Mahābhārata*, the *Bhāgavatapurāṇa*, the *Vāsiṣṭhasmṛti*, the *Paithīnasīsmṛti*, and a Tamil text *Tiruvilaiyatara purāṇam* give us the same myth with some variations here and there. *Prayogapārijāta* also quotes some *purāṇa* citations which narrate the same myth. Thus, in this context the TS is the source of these texts. All these texts unanimously agree upon one thing that women have accepted a certain portion of Indra's sin and it was transformed into menstrual flow. However, these texts differ on certain points.

Brahmahatyā or Bhrūṇahatyā

Except *Vāsiṣṭha-Smṛti* (VS) and *Paithīnasī-Smṛti* (PS) all these texts narrate that mestruation is the manifestation of Brahmanicide. However, these two texts tell that it is a manifestation of infanticide.

VS 5.8 स स्त्रिय उपाधावत् । अस्यै मे भ्रूणहत्यायै तृतीयं भागं प्रतिगृहीत' इति......सैषा भ्रूणहत्या मासि मासि आविर्भवति ।

PS तं देवा भ्रूणहन्नित्यवदन् । स स्त्रिय उपादधथीत । अस्यै भ्रूणहत्यायै तृतीयं भागं प्रतिगृहीत वरं दास्यामीति ।

Here, one can say that in these texts the word *bhrūṇahatyā* is a slip of the pen. (i) Because in the PS we get both versions भ्रूणहत्या and ब्रह्महत्या. It says further, ततोऽशं तृतीयं ब्रह्महत्याया: स्त्रिय: प्रपद्यन्ते । etc. (ii) Secondly, we cannot call Viśvarūpa who was the priest of Gods as भ्रूण i.e. an infant. (iii) In many *Dharmaśāstra* texts menstruation is associated with infanticide. If husband does not approach his wife in ऋतुकाल or if father does not arrange for her marriage after her puberty, they both are accused of infanticide. Because of such impressions only the authors of these *Smṛtis* might have noted the word भ्रूणहत्या instead of ब्रह्महत्या ।This is the first point of difference.

2. Secondly, these texts differ in the name of persons killed by Indra. As per the account given in these texts we can say that Indra was accused of Brahminicide twice.

1. Firstly, when, he had slaughtered Viśvarūpa
2. Secondly, when he had killed Vṛtra.

The *Bhāgavatapurāṇa*, the *Skandapurāṇa*, the above quoted two *Smṛtis* and the *Tiruvilaiyatarapurāṇam* relate menstruation to the slaughter of Viśvarūpa keeping in front the account of the TS. Whereas the *Mahābhārata* and the *Rāmāyaṇa* relate it to the slaughter of Vṛtra.

3. Thirdly, these texts vary in the number and names of the recipients of the sin.

The TS tells us that Brahmanicide was divided into three portions and given to the Earth, trees and women. The above texts give us different accounts. Let us discuss them one by one.

According to the *Rāmayaṇa* (R) Brahminicide divided itself into four parts and took resort to four things (i) rivers (ii) trees (iii) women and (iv) those persons who kill brahmins. To quote,

चतुर्धा विभजात्मानमात्मनैव दूरासदे ।
देवानां भाषितं श्रुत्वा ब्रह्महत्त्या महात्मनाम् ॥
सन्निधौ स्थानमन्यत्र वरयामास दुर्वसा ।
एकेनांशेन वत्स्यामि पूर्णोदासु नदीषु वै ॥
द्वितीयेन तु वृक्षेषु सत्यमेतद् ब्रवीमि वः ।
योऽयमंशस्तृतीयो मे स्त्रीषु यौवनशालिषु ॥
हन्तारो ब्राह्मणान्ये तु प्रेक्षापूर्वमदूषकान् ।
तांश्चतुर्थेन भागेन संश्रयिष्ये सुरर्षभाः ॥

(*Rāmāyaṇa* 7.77.11-15)

According to the *Mahābhārata (Śāntiparvan)*[5] Agni, trees, Apsaras and water are the four recipients of the sin. These transmit the sin to the following persons :

(1) *Brahmahatyā* in Agni catches a person who does not perform sacrifice.
(2) Brahmanicide in trees clings to a person who cuts them in *Parvakāla*.
(3) It, residing in Apsaras finds her place in that person who approaches a menstruating lady.
(4) It, residing in water catches a person who throws dirt in waters.

This text directly does not label menstruation as the transformed state of Brahmanicide. However, it marks it as a sin when one approaches such a lady.

The *Bhāgavatapurāṇa*[6] does not differ much from the TS, only it adds one member to the list of recipients enlisted in the TS. It says.

संवत्सरान्ते तदघं भूतानां स विशुद्धये ।
भूम्यम्बुद्रुमयोषिद्भ्य यश्चतुर्धा-भजद्धरिः ॥
भूमिस्तुरीयं जग्राह श्वातपूरवरेण वै ।
ईरिणं ब्रह्महत्यायाः रूपं भूमौ प्रदृश्यते ॥
तुर्यं छेदविरोधेण वरेण जग्रहुर्द्रुमाः ।
तेषां निर्यासरूपेण ब्रह्महत्या प्रदृश्यते ॥

शश्वत्कामवरेणाहंस्तृतीयं जग्रहु: स्त्रिय: ।
रजोरूपेण तांस्वंहो मासि मासि प्रदृश्यते ॥
द्रव्यभूयोवरेणापस्तुरीयं जग्रहुर्मलम् ।
तासु बुद् बुदफेनाभ्यां हृष्टं तद्धरति क्षिपन् ॥

The *Skandapurāṇa* (SKP) *Revākhaṇḍa*[7] describes the four members in the following manner. Brahma divides the sin into water, earth, women, and a Brahmin who is doing the duties of a *Vaiśya* and *Śūdra*. Since the sin is divided among these, there are certain restrictions.

The SKP describes :

अवगाह्य तत: पेया: आपो वै नान्यथा बुधै: ।
अभक्ष्या तेन सञ्जाता सदाकालं वसुन्धरा ।
असंग्राह्या त्वसंग्राह्या तेन जाता रजस्वला ॥

118, 28-32

The *Māheśvarakhaṇḍa* of the SKP also describes that Bṛhaspati had distributed the sin among the Earth, trees, waters and women. The boons given in return to these are as follows :

For the Earth :

यदा यदुकुले श्रीमान् वासुदेवो भविष्यति ।
तदा तत्पदविन्यासान्निष्पापा त्वं भविष्यसि ॥

For trees :

छेदिताश्चैव सर्वे वै त्यनेकांशत्वमागता: ।
ततो विटपिनो नित्यं यूयं सर्वे भविष्यथ ॥३६ ॥

For waters :

मा भयं क्रियतामाप एनसा दुस्तरेण हि ।
आप: पुनन्तु सर्वेषां चराचरनिवासिनाम् ॥३७ ॥

For women :

मा भयं क्रियतां सर्वा: पापादस्मात् सुलोचना: ।
भविष्याणां तथान्येषां भविष्यति फलप्रद: ॥३८ ॥
हत्त्यांशो यो हि सर्वासां यथाकामित्वमेव च ।

(*Kedārakhaṇḍa*, 15th *Adhyāya*)

For the details of a parallel story in *Tiruvilaiyapurāṇam* (1.12 - 14) I quote O 'Flaherty.[9] She says - " In a Tamil text, the same four recipients have the sin of Viśvarūpa's murder, released from them in the very form in which it is said to appear in them in several Sanskrit texts. It flows out of women in their monthly period, out of water in disgusting foam, out of trees in their sap and out of the earth in the salt soil. Thus, it will come out and vanish. In addition, the four receptacles are given boons as in the Sanskrit texts and the sin when Indra comes to the shrine of Śiva."

Thus, from these versions of the myth we can say :

(i) The myth of the TS is the source book of these versions.

(ii) Though these texts do not go hand in hand regarding the recipients of the sin, all these texts strongly say that women have accepted a portion of Brahminicide and it flows out of them in each month.

With this background now we should turn to the main part of the paper, i.e. observations.

Observations

From this myth and its versions in the Indian texts, it can be observed that this particular myth strongly puts forth that menstruation is the manifestation of the greatest sin i.e. *Brahmahatyā*.[11] Labeling menstruation as the direct outcome of *brahmahatyā* is the main purport of the myth. It wants to stress the association between this particular bodily phenomenon and the most horrible sin which the people could imagine.

It will not be unwise here to quote some parallel myths which show the association between menstruation and sin.

The *Mārkaṇḍeya Purāṇa*[12] describes the first human creation by Brahma, Brahma created one thousand couples of each *varṇa* i.e. *Brāhmaṇa, Kṣatriya, Vaiśya* and *Śūdra*, from his mouth, chest, thigh, and feet respectively. In this *Maithunakalpa* though men and women used to meet, they were not getting any progeny. Because there was no menstrual flow among women. Only at the end of their life they used to give birth to only two children Kulaka and Kulikā. In those days people did not have desire and therefore they were always happy. It says :

मासि मासि आर्तवं यत्तु न तदासीत्तु योषिताम् ।
तस्मात्तदा न षुषुवुः सेवितैरपि मैथुनैः ॥
आयुषोन्ते प्रसूयन्ते मिथुनान्येवताः सकृत् ।
कुलिकं कुलिकां चैव उत्पाद्यन्ते मुमुर्षताम् ॥
ततः प्रभृति कल्पेऽस्मिन् मिथुनानां हि सम्भवः ।
ता वै निष्कामचारिण्यो नित्यं मुदितमानसाः ॥

अन्योन्यं हृच्छयाविष्टा मैथुनायोपचक्रमुः ॥

Adhyāya 41

But thereafter, without any cause, lustful passion arose and because of it women began to menstruate, they conceived again and again. Since the unending passion arose, the *Kalpavṛkṣas* around their natural surroundings destroyed and people started hating one another, ceasing belongings of others and created bounded surroundings etc. Thus, the menstruation and other faults in human character are the results of lustful passion.

ततः कालेन वै रागः तथाऽकस्मिकोऽभवत् ।
मासि वा आर्तवोत्पत्त्या गर्भोत्पत्तिः पुनः पुनः ।
रागोत्पत्त्या ततस्तासां वृक्षस्ते गृहंसंस्थिताः ।
प्रणेशु..... etc.

Thus, the narration of creation of human beings links menstruation with lustful passion and in Indian thinking such passion has sinful nature. This link between menstruation and passion is certainly parallel to the association of the same with Brahmanicide.

While describing evil forces in the world *Mārkaṇḍeya Purāṇa* says:[13] Nirti and Alakṣmī are the two wives of Death. From Alkaṣmī he got fourteen sons, including Duḥsaha. Duḥsaha married Nimārṣṭi. She was born to Kali's wife when she saw a *Cāṇḍāla* at the time of menstruation. From Nimārṣṭi, Duḥsaha got eight sons and eight daughters. *Gaṇḍaprāntarati* was his sixth son. He got six sons who took resort to a person who approaches his wife at the initial four days of her period, 13th day, 11th day, at day time, at *paran* and on *Śrāddha* day. Therefore, one should not meet her on such days, because it is a time for the progeny of *Gaṇḍaprantarati*. This narration also supports the statement that menstruation was viewed in association with evil forces which definitely have some relation with sin.

Apart from these *Purāṇic* myths which show relation between menstruation and sin or similar evil things, I may quote a tribal legend which relates menstruation to a sinful act. Gonds, a tribe in Satpura hills say:[14]

Doganguru had seven daughters, who were fairies in water. These used to create some kind of diseases among people. Therefore, these were kept locked in a room. Once Mahādeva and Pārvatī stayed in the house wherein these fairies were kept locked. While going out Mahādeva ordered Pārvatī not to open the seventh room. Out of curiosity Pārvatī opened that room and these daughters of Doganguru entered in her womb. Because of them she underwent painful situations like menstruation, pregnancy, delivery etc. As Pārvatī represents the woman class all other women also have to undergo these.

According to Gonds twenty-one *Prithivi* goddesses and seven watery fairies possess a sinful person in the form of some disease. Menstruation is caused by them because of the sinful act of Pārvatī i.e. disobeying the order of Śiva.

This legend reminds us of another belief in Turkish society - "Menstruation is believed to have been given to women because of Hawa's (of Eve) act of disobedience against Allah in Cennet (Garden/Paradise)".[15]

All these references are clear enough to mark the association between menstruation and sin or sinful act. Once this association is clear, the immediate question which comes to our mind is: what could be the reason behind such association? What prompted people to link these two things?

It is possible that sudden coming of enormous blood reminded them of killing and killing is the most terrible sin on the earth and as a punishment for such a sin seclusion of women was prescribed. Many tribals all around the globe construct special menstruation huts in which such women are secluded. The period for seclusion differs from culture to culture. I can quote a few examples. In South India women of *Pantaram* and *Kaliyan* tribes are secluded for 16 and 15 days respectively in special menstrual huts. *Maduvana* and *Mannam* tribal women use menstrual huts for three and four days respectively. Urali women use hollow of the tree as menstrual hut.[16] Hindu Dharmaśāstra texts prescribe 3/4 days seclusion for such ladies. In Avestan Pahlavi text *Ārmestgāh* are mentioned. These denote a special room for a menstruating woman where food and other things are to be kept from a distance by means of a stick.[17]

Such seclusion of women for a particular period shows that she was punished by the people for that particular period. She was called चाण्डाली etc.,[18] and communication with her was prohibited. The tale of Gonds also says that the seven Apsaras were locked in a room. These were locked because people had strong hatred for menstruation etc., which reminded them of killing.

Another, strong hatred for menstruation might be because of the fear of blood especially that of menstrual blood. Sudden flow of blood from the genital of women is certainly a fearful thing on the part of a person who had zero knowledge of human physiology. It is possible that they knew only two-three reasons behind any blood flow.

(a) because of sharp weapons or injuries.

(b) because of the bites of beasts or reptiles.[19]

However, one cannot point out to any such reason behind menstrual bleeding. Moreover, this bleeding was monthly. Thus, it is an obvious case of fright for a person who fears from any kind of bleeding. Thus, sudden bleeding and regular occurrence of it are the two reasons to label menstruation as of perilous nature. Therefore, people of various primitive societies looked at it as a fearful thing. This fear prompted them to seclude women.

This fear of blood has shadowed even the myth under discussion. The following points will highlight how the fear of blood is the central theme of the myth.

Indra had divided the sin into three parts. Earth, plants and women had shared the sin. The portion of sin accepted by the recipients was transformed into something perceivable.

In case of the Earth it is ईरिण i.e. naturally barren land. It is to be avoided because it bears the colour of *Brahmahatyā*. Though the word ईरिण is unanimously interpreted as a barren land, non-fertile land, in this context, I think the land in the mind of author of the myth is that non-fertile land which bears red or reddish colour. There are many types of *Iriṇas* i.e. sandy land . अपां कृतमिरिणम्, स्वकृतइरिण means naturally barren land. However, in the above quoted legend it may be that barren land which bears reddish colour, i.e. the colour of *Brahmahatyā*. The legend says ब्रह्महत्यायै एष वर्णः । *Prayogapārijāta*[20] quotes some Purāṇa citation which also stresses that i.e. sap, resemble blood. It says :

ईरिणं न स्पृशेत्तस्मात् ब्रह्महत्यासवर्णकम्
सोऽभवत् रक्तनिर्यासो ब्रह्महत्या सवर्णकः ॥
तस्माल्लोहितनिर्यासं न स्पृशेन्न च श्वादयेत् ।

In case of plants Brahmanicide was transformed to resin or gum. It should not be eaten because it bears red colour. The legend further says, it may bear red colour or any other colour, whatever occurs should not be eaten. सः निर्यासः अभवत् । तस्मात् निर्यासस्य न आश्यम् । ब्रह्महत्यायै हि एष वर्णः । अथ खलु यः एव लोहितः यः वा आव्रश्चनात् निर्येषति तस्य न आश्यम् ।

Thirdly, in case of women it is actual blood that is released from her body. Thus, all these three objects are forbidden because these possess blood or resemble blood actually or symbolically. It is the association of the above things with blood which prompted Vedic persons to link these with sin.

Frazer in his *'The Golden Bough'*[21] rightly remarks - "The motive for the restraints so commonly imposed on girls at puberty is the deeply engrained dread which primitive man universally entertains of menstrual blood. He fears it all times but especially on its first appearance."

The fear of blood is echoed variously in various tribes. I may quote a few beliefs regarding this which are quoted by Frazer.

(1) "In West Succex people believe that the ground on which human blood has been shed is accursed and will remain barren for ever. (Compare here ईरिण has come into existence when the Earth accepted the ब्रह्महत्या i.e. when she was covered with blood of Brahmin.)

(2) "Among the Latuka of Central Africa and earth on which a drop of blood has fallen at childbirth is carefully scrapped up with an iron shovel, put into a pot along with the water used in washing the mother and buried tolerably deep outside the house on the left side."

(3) "In West Africa, if a drop of your blood has fallen on the ground, you must carefully cover it up, rub and stamp it into the soil. It is on the side of canol or a tree. The place is cut out and the chip destroyed.

(ii) Since blood, especially menstrual blood was thought to be of perilous nature it was linked with fearful beings such as witches, ghosts etc., and therefore it has a prominent role in witchcraft.

In this context we can point out to a chain of homicides at Manvat in the last decade. For obtaining hidden treasure girls having their first puberty were killed.

Mantramahodadhi[22] - a Tantra text gives some ritual in which menstrual blood is used for fulfilling certain desires.

If a person worships Simukhī in the mystic diagram with certain *mantras* and performs *Homa* with a cloth smeared with the menstrual flow of a woman, honey and milk pudding he can control mob.

If a person worships Chinnamastā, through a proper ritual, he will obtain all desired objects. Ability to influence and attract people is obtained if the menstrual blood is used in rituals.

(iii) As it was linked with persons of demonic nature because of its perilous nature, similarly because of its impurity which the people imagined, it was linked with demon. Primitive people thought that menstrual blood pollutes the surrounding and a menstruous woman contaminates other people and object. Therefore one should not eat anything given by her and since it was thought to be impure, purification ceremonies follow. The association between impurity and demon is found in many cultures. It is a belief that if one does not wash feet *Kali* possess him. Secondly, it was also believed that eveything that does out of the body of man is dead and impure, and immediately becomes property of demon. The cut off nails, hairs, and teeth are impure and therefore one should take bath after cutting and the objects such as nails should be destroyed. According to *Avesta*, the menses which are unclean are sent by Ahriman, especially when the last beyond the usual period. Therefore, a woman, as long as they last is unclean and therefore possessed of the demon. Many tribal women immediately destroy the linen used with the fear that it should not fall into the hands of a demon witch or a magician.

Thus, since the primitive man was afraid of the sudden oozing of blood and since he considered it impure it was linked with black magic. And to avoid the replications of witchcraft etc., he thought of keeping away from it and therefore secluded such women.

Though these people were very much afraid of menstruation, they came to know the relation between the cease of mestruation and pregnancy. Therefore, though the actual state was not desired, however the results of it were very much desired. Slowly he came to know that it is a state because of which a girl becomes mature to bear progeny. Therefore, the first puberty is celebrated in many cultures. In the legend under discussion the progeny and sexual pleasures are considered as boons received by women in return of the acceptance of the sin and the things which beget progeny are involved in it. Earth bears crops, plants grow and get fruit and women get children.

Concluding Remarks

The myth under discussion interprets menstruation as the manifestation of sin. This was due to the fear of blood. Such fear arouse in the primitive mind because of the sudden and regular flow of blood in women. Because of its perilous and unclean nature it acted as an instrument in witchraft. Therefore they found a way out to avoid it and it was seclusion. When they came to know the relation between menstruation and procreation puberty rites were introduced.

It is also a possibility that when the primitive man came to know the association of menses and progeny, protection of such women became necessary since all primitive tribes care for procreation and as a remedy to protect her, restrictions tightened. However, from the present myth one cannot observe such a relation.

Thus, here I have presented the rationale which the primitive mind might have had in its front.

REFERENCES

1. *Taittirīya Saṁhitā* Vol. II, pt. I (*Kāṇḍa* II) Ed. Dharmadhikari, T.N. & Athlekar, S.L., Vaidik Samshodhan Mandal, Pune, 1981.
2. In such narrations many a times brahmanicide is personified e.g. *Mahābhārata* describes it as:

   ब्रह्महत्या महाघोरा रौद्रा लोकभयावहा ॥
   करालदशना भीमा विकृता कृष्णपिङ्गला ।
   प्रकीर्णमूर्धजा चैव घोरनेत्रा च भारत ।
   कपालमालिनी चैव कृशा च भरतर्षभा ।
   रुधिरार्द्रा च धर्मज्ञ चीरवस्त्रनिवासिनी ।

   (*MBh.* 12.273. 10b - 12)
3. The verses quoted in the *Saṁskārakāṇḍa* of *Dharmakośa* (Vol. III, pt. IV) Wai, 1983 are utilised here.
4. *The Vālmikī Rāmāyaṇa* (ed), Shah, U.P. Oriental Institute, Baroda, 1975.

5. *The Śāntiparvan* pt. III, A) Ed. Belvalkar, S.K., BORI, Poona, 1954.
6. *Śrimadbhāgavatapurāṇam* with Sanskrit com. of Śrīdharaswāmin ed. Shastri, Jagoshlal, Motilal Banarasidass, Delhi, 1983.
7. *Skandapurāṇam*, Vol. 5 (*Uttarārdham*) Gurumandal Series No. XX, Calcutta, 1962.
8. *Śrīskandamahāpurāṇam* I (*Māheśvarakhaṇḍa*) Ed. Nag Sharan Singh, Nag Publications, Delhi, 1981.
9. O Flaherty, *'The Origin of Evil in Hindu Mytholgy'*, Motilal Banarasidass, Delhi, 1976, pp. 157-158.
10. *Brahmahatyā* is described as one of the greatest sins in almost all Smṛtis. As a token I quote:
    ब्रह्महा च सुरापश्च तस्करो गुरुतल्पगः ।
    एते सर्वे पृथक् ज्ञेया महापातकिनो नराः ॥ Manu, 9.235
11. The *Mārkaṇḍeya Purāṇa*, Vol. I, *Adhyāya* 41. Ed. Pt. Srirama Sharma Acharya, Bareli, 1967.
12. *Ibid*, Adhyāya 43.
    दुःसहस्याभवद्भार्या निमार्ष्टिर्नाम नामतः ।
    जाता कलेस्तु भार्यायामृतौ चाण्डालदर्शनात् ॥२ ॥ etc.
13. *Ibid*. *Adhyāya* 43. 746-77...
    षडपत्यानि कथ्यन्ते गण्डप्रान्तरतेस्तथा ।
    स्त्रीणां रजस्यवस्थानं तेषां कालांश्च मे शृणु ॥
    चत्वार्य्यहानि पूर्वाणि तथैवान्यत्त्रयोदशम् ।
    एकादशं तथैवान्यदपत्यं तस्य वै दिने ।
    दिनाभिगमने श्राद्धदिने तथापरे
    पर्ग्वास्वथान्यत्तस्मात्तु वर्ज्यान्येतानि पण्डितैः ॥etc.
14. *Dharma ani Lokasahitya* (Marathi) Durga, Bhagwat, Popular Prakashan, Bombay, 1975.
15. Carol Delaney, "Menstruation in Turkish Village Society" in *"Anthropology of Menstruation"*
16. *Rajaḥkaṇa* (Marathi) Chapekar, N.G. Pune, 1922.
17. *Encyclopaedia of Religion and Ethics*, Vol. 10, p. 492b. (Ed. by James Hastings).
18. प्रथमेऽहनि चाण्डाली यथा वर्ज्या तथाङ्गना ।
    द्वितीयेऽहनि विज्ञेया यथा वै ब्रह्मघातिनी ।
    तृतीये वृषली ज्ञेया चतुर्थेऽहनि शुद्ध्यति
    लिङ्गपुराणम्, 109-110
19. This is shown by images from New Guinea in which a crocodile or snake enters or emerges from the female organ etc. see *Encyclopaedia* of *Religion and Ethics*, Vol. II, pp. 411.
20. Quoted in the *Saṁskārakāṇḍa*, Vol. III. pt. IV of *Dharmakośa*, Wai, 1983.
21. *The Golden Bough*, (Abb. ed.) Frazer, James, George, London, 1963.
22. *Mantramahodadhi* (Tr.) Indian Book Centre, Delhi.

19

THE VARIETIES OF ARTHĀPATTI : THE STAND OF THE PRĀBHĀKARA SCHOOL

K.N. Hota

About the varieties of *arthāpatti* there continues a big dispute between the Bhāṭṭas and the Prābhākaras. In the definition of *Arthāpatti* (i.e., *dṛṣṭaḥ śruto vārthonyathā nopapadyate ityarthakalpanā*),[1] Śabara simply mentions the words *'dṛṣṭa'* and *'śruta'* which became the main source for the Bhāṭṭas to divide *arthāpatti* into two forms as *dṛṣṭārtāpatti* 'presumption from the seen fact' and *śrutārthāpatti* 'presumption from the heard fact'. They claim that Śabara had the idea of the above two forms of *arthāpatti* and this is the reason why he writes the words *'dṛṣṭa* and *'śruta'* in the definition. In this connection, we may not agree with the Bhāṭṭas, who hold two forms of *arthāpatti* on the ground that Śabara has given only one example of *arthāpatti*. But in that case, if he had an intention of two forms of *arthāpatti*, he should have given two examples instead of one. However, the Bhāṭṭas again subdivide *dṛṣṭārthāpatti* into five forms and including the *śrutārthāpatti* they have six divisions or forms of *arthāpatti* in all. In the present discussion, our main focus is on the first two varieties of *arthāpatti*.

According to the Bhāṭṭas, in case of *dṛṣṭārthāpatti*, when the seen or known fact, viz. living Devadatta is absent from his house, becomes inexplicable, there we presume another fact, viz. he exists outside (the house). Likewise, in case of *śrutārthāpatti*, when the sentence which is heard, remains inexplicable, what one presumes is the words or sentence. As for example, *pīno devadattaḥ divā na bhuṅkte* 'Devadatta is fat, but does not take food during the day'. After hearing this sentence, when one finds the inexplicability of two clauses, i.e., fatness and non-eating by the day, he presumes the word *rātribhojana* 'he eats at night', but not its fact. To substantiate their stand, they quote a maxim which explains that the expectancy of words is fulfilled by words only (*śābdī hyākāṅkṣā śabdenaiva prapūryate*).[2] So when a sentence is inexplicable, one has to presume the sentence or words only, but not its meaning. This is the stand of the Bhāṭṭas for maintaining *śrūtārthāpatti*.

Prabhākara criticizes the Bhāṭṭas' account of two forms of *arthāpatti*. While interpreting Śabara's *Bhāṣya* he tells that both the words *'dṛṣṭa'* and *'śruta'* are used here in the sense of object that is known (*upalabdhorthaḥ*). Mere difference between these two words here lies in naming only. So one should not be under the impression that these two words stand for different purpose.[3] Śālikanātha opines that by accepting *upalabdha* we not only include the perceptual cognition or the verbal cognition but also include all such cognitions like inferential cognition etc.[4] That means the object on which *arthāpatti* is based on, can be known by any of the *pramāṇas* accepted in the system. From the above points it is clearly evident that Śabara didn't have the idea of classifying *arthāpatti* in two forms as the Bhāṭṭas intend.

While repudiating *śrutārthāpatti*, Prabhākara contends that after the verbal cognition of *pīno devadattaḥ divā na bhuṅkte*, what is actually presumed is the fact or *artha* (object) *rātribhojana* 'eating at night', but not the word *rātribhojana*. Without the postulation of fact *rātribhojana* what remains inexplicable is *pīno devadattaḥ* etc. and this inexplicability is subsided only by the presumption of the fact, *rātribhojana* and hence, in this case, the words or the sentence cannot be presumed.[5] In support of this view, Rāmānujācārya tells that the expectancy of the words is subsided by the relation of the object postulated also (*śābdī hyākāṅkṣā kalpitārthānvayenāpi śāmyati*).[6]

Here, the Bhāṭṭas try to establish *śrutārthāpatti* with the help of determinate cognition (*savikalpakajñāna*). They are of the opinion that since the object has a determinate cognition, and since the determinate cognition is expressed by words, there is no difficulty, if one presumes words in order to remove the inexplicability (*anupapatti*). Because the word which is presumed, can also remind its object (*sa ca śabdassvārtham-upasthāpayati*).[7]

But, Śālikanātha rejects this view and replies that it is not true that all cognitions are determinate cognitions and so also they are determined by words. Cognition can be either of determinate (*savikalpaka*) or of indeterminate (*nirvikalpaka*). It is a fact that a word can reveal its object at the stage of determinate cognition, but it is not so when there is an indeterminate cognition. For example, when the sense-organ (in perception) and the probans (in inference for one-self, i.e., *svārthānumāna*) generates mere knowledge of object, the word plays no role to express its object. Because it is such a stage where one knows mere object only. So, the attempt made by the Bhāṭṭas for establishing *śrutārthāpatti* stands completely futile.[8]

Further, one may argue that as *dṛṣṭārtha* 'the object that is heard' is the postulating ground of *dṛṣṭārthāpatti, śrutārtha* (the object that is heard) can also be the postulating factor' of *śrutārthāpatti.*[9] Śālikanātha does not agree with this opinion. He replies that whatever cognition becomes the removing factor of *anupapatti* the same is to be treated as the ground for *arthāpatti*. In this state, if *anupapatti* is removed even by the words there would be no objection to account *śabda* (i.e. *śrutārtha*) as the ground for *arthāpatti.*[10] However, in *pīno devadattaḥ* etc., we do not have any cognition about one's eating that is related to night (*rātrisambandhe hi bhojanasyānavagate*) and this is the reason that *anupapatti* arises in *rātribhojana*. Such *anupapatti* cannot be eliminated by mere cognition of words, since those words like eating at night are incapable of producing the fact '*bhojanasya rātrisambandhaḥ*'.[11]

Another difficulty that has been raised by Śālikanātha in *śrutārthāpatti* is that if mere words will be presumed in *arthāpatti*, then, in those cases where the meaning of words is not known, there, even after the presumption of words, the inexplicability cannot be removed. Thus, after uttering the sentence '*pīno devadattaḥ divā na bhuṅkte*, if it is uttered *yāminyām atti* meaning 'eats at night' then a person who does not know the meaning of those words '*yāminī*' and '*atti*' cannot resolve the inexplicability that arises after uttering the sentence '*pīno devadattaḥ* etc.'[12] So, in all cases of *arthāpatti*, it is necessary to presume the object or the fact, but not its words.

Conclusion

A close examination of the Prābhākara view would reveal that the case of *śrutārthāpatti* is not different from *dṛṣṭārthāpatti*. In *arthāpatti*, the conflict or inexplicability is actually removed by the presumption of the fact. After presuming the fact, one can express it through the words, but if words would be presumed then a person who is not aware of about the relation between the word and its meaning, cannot be successful to remove the inexplicability. Finally, Prabhākara concludes that *śrutārthāpatti* cannot be treated as a variety of *arthāpatti*, since it is subsumed under the *dṛṣṭārthāpatti*. Moreover, if *śrutārthāpatti* is accepted, the authenticity of Veda will be at stake. Because, the sentence which is postulated is the human-sentence and its authenticity is always subject of doubt.

REFERENCES

1. *Śābarabhāṣya* on *Sūtra* 1.1.5.
2. *Tantrarahasya* of Rāmānujācārya, Edited by Shastry, R. Sharma, Oriental Institute, Baroda, 2nd edn. 1956, p. 13.
3. *Dṛṣṭaḥ śruto vā iti darśana- śravaṇopanyāsaḥ kiṁ kāraṇāntara-vyudāsāya? Neti vadāmaḥ, upalabdho'rthaḥ-ityarthaḥ. Śrutagrahaṇam idānīm kimartham? "Dṛṣṭaḥ" ity eva vaktavyam. Ucyate- abhidhānāntaram evedam - "dṛṣṭaḥ śruto vā" ity- upalabdher vācakam. Bṛhatī*, Edited by Sastri S.K. Ramanatha, University of Madras, 1934, p. 115.
4. *Tataścopalabdha-mātra-grahaṇāt sarvapramāṇa- saṁgrahobh-avatītyarthaḥ, Ṛjuvimalāpañcikā*, a commentary on *Bṛhatī, Ibid.*, p. 115.
5. *Tad ayuktam. Atrāpyarthasyaiva kalpayitumucitatvāt. Yasmin hy akalpite' nupapattiḥ tadarthāpattyā pratīyate. Rātrisambandhe hyanavagate bhojanasyā'nupapattiḥ, Prakaraṇapañcikā (Pra Pañ)*, Edited by Sastri, A. Subrahmanya and Murti, T.R.V., Banaras Hindu University Darshana Series No. 4, Banaras, 1961, p. 279.
6. Shastry, *Op.cit.*, p. 13.
7. *Athocyate - arthasadbhāvam eva kalpayitum arthāpattiḥ pravartamānā tasyā' rthasya savikalpaka-jñānavedyatvāt, savikalpaka-jñānānāñca śabdapurassaratvāt purovarttini śabda evā' rthāpattiḥ paryavasyati, sa ca śabdas-svārtham upasthāpayati, Pra Pañ*, p. 279.
8. *Na cedam āśaṅkanīyam-laiṅgikam aindriyakañca sarvam eva savikalpakaṁ śabda evā'nena nyāyena paryavasyed iti. Yato nirvikalpakadaśāyām indriyasya liṅgasya cārthabodha eva sāmarthyam dṛśyate, tena savikalpakāvasthāyām apy artha eva tayor vyāpāraḥ parikalpyate. Śrutārthāpattibodhastu nirvikalpako na sambhavati, śabdavyutpattipūrvakatvāt, Ibid.*, pp. 279-80.
9. *Atrocyate - dṛṣṭārthāpattāu artha evā' arthāpatteḥ pramāṇatvaṁ dṛṣṭam iti, śrutārthāpatter-api tatraiva prāmāṇyaṁ syād iti, Ibid.*, p. 280.
10. *Tan na. yasmin khalv avagate' nupapattis śāmyati, tatrā' rthāpatteḥ prāmāṇyam. Śabde' pi cā'vagate śāmyaty evānupapattiḥ, atastatrā'pi prāmāṇyam nā' yuktam iti, Ibid.*
11. *Atrocyate - rātrisambandhe hi bhojanasyā' navagate' nupapattir āpatati. Sā, tāvacchabdasvarūpamātre' vagate' pi na śāmyati, yāvat tatśabdād-rātrisambandho bhojanasya nā' vagamyate, Ibid.*
12. *Na hi "pīno devadatto divā na bhuṅka" iti prayujya yadā punar evam ucyate - yāminyām attīti, tadā yāminī - śabde, attau cā'vyutpannasya pūrvavākyātha viṣayā' nupapattir uparamati. Ato' rthasyaiva sākṣād upapādakatvam, na śabdasya, Ibid.*

20

PRAMĀṆA—MĪMĀṀSĀ

A Ramanna

A means of knowledge is defined as the collection of all the conditions of right knowledge. Jaimini, the Sūtrakāra, employs the three attributes, viz., (1) absence of defects in the source (*Autpattika*), (2) absence of contradictory knowledge (*Avyatireka*) and (3) previously unacquired (*Arthe'nupalabhdhe*)[1] to the means of Dharma. Hence it is clear that the constituents of a means of knowledge are absence of defects in the source, absence of contradiction and the apprehension of that which was not previously known.

According to Śabarasvāmin, the Bhāṣyakāra, consciousness is the means of knowledge but, unlike the Buddhist, he holds that the result produced by the means of knowledge is different from the means itself. This result is knownness (*Jñātatā*) of the object.

The Buddhist gives definition of means of knowledge as 'a non-contradicted experience of an object hitherto uncognised' (*Anadhigatārthādhigantṛ pramāṇam avisaṁvādi jñānam*).[2] The criticism of Kumārila and his followers is directed against the Buddhist view that this definition is too comprehensive (*Ativyāpta*) and too narrow (*Avyāpta)* as it includes some cases of memory and excludes inferential knowledge of past and future objects under right knowledge because, some cases of memory possess efficiency and the inferential knowledge lack practical efficiency.[3]

The Naiyāyika defines means of knowledge as, 'the instrument of knowledge' (*pramākaraṇam pramāṇam*).[4] Even though there is no dispute about the definition but, we can see a controversy over the validity of restatement. The Naiyāyika does not accept validity to restatements. According to him it does not possess any difference from the previous knowledge either in the determination of facts or in emperical usage. Hence it should not be included in right knowledge. But the Bhāṭṭa accepts validity of restatements like continuous streams of knowledge (*Dhārāvāhikajñāna*).

I. Bhāṭṭa View

Kumārila Bhaṭṭa defines means of knowledge as that knowledge which is a means in enabling us to apprehend that 'special luminosity' (*Prakāśaviśeṣa*) which abides in the objects apprehended.[5] Pārthasārathi says that what constitutes means of knowledge is the knowledge of that which is not contradicted by a subsequent experience and which relates to something not previously apprehended (*Kāraṇadoṣabādhakajñānarahitam, agṛhītagrāhi jñānaṁ pramāṇaṁ*).[6] One may ask that in a continuous stream of knowledge (*Dhārāvāhika jñāna*) (referring to the same object), we have fixing our attention on the object, different intellections of the same object, e.g. 'this is a book and so on'; the intellections that are subsequent to that which is the first member of the series are merely a repetition and as such they (the later ones' cease to be valid. Reply of the Bhāṭṭas to this is that, even there, there is the knowledge of each succeeding element of time like, this', which was unknown, and because the existence of the book in the succeeding moment is not understood by the previous knowledge.[7] The Bhāṭṭa accepts six means of right knowledge. These are : perception (*Pratyakṣa*), inference (*Anumāna*), verbal testimony (*Śabda*), analogy (*Upamāna*), presumption (*Arthāpatti*) and non-apprehension (*Anupalabdhi*). The Materialist (*Cārvāka*) recognises only one means of right knowledge, viz., perception.[8] He rejects the validity of inference on the ground that there is not sufficient warrant for believing in the truth of the pervasion (*vyāpti*) which forms its basis. But this argument stultifies the Materialist's own position. His conclusion that 'inference is not valid' is itself the result of induction, and points to a conviction that in one case, at least, the relation of pervasion holds true.

Buddhists say that as there are only two kinds of objects, so there can be only two kinds of means of right knowledge to grasp each of them. And there is not third kind of object in addition to perceptible and imperceptible. There can be nothing which is neither perceptible nor imperceptible. Perception is able to grasp perceptible objects, and inference can grasp imperceptible. Hence, only two means of knowledge.[9] Vaiśeṣikas also accept only two *pramāṇas*. They include verbal testimony in inference. Their argument is that in the form of an inference in which the words or the meanings of words in a sentence form the subject (*pakṣa*); the connection of meanings remembered through those words form the probandum (*Sādhya*); on expectancy, etc., forms the reason; even sentence forms the example.[10] Putting forward this inference, the Vaiśeṣika argues that the verbal testimony can be had through inference. But the Bhāṭṭa refutes this argument by pointing out dissimilar knowledge that arises respectively through inference and word. If the argument of the Vaiśeṣikas that verbal testimony also arises through inference, then the knowledge that arises through inference must be 'I know this by inference'. But this is dissimilar to the knowledge that arises among people, for, it is observed that one gets the notion, 'I know this through verbal testimony', whenever verbal knowledge is gained. Therefore, verbal knowledge is a distinct means of knowledge.

Sāṁkhyas and Bhāsarvajña accept three means of right knowledge, viz., perception, inference and verbal testimony. Other means of knowledge noted by other philosophers, according to Bhāsarvajña, could be included of four under these three[11] *Pramāṇas*. He argues later with great ingenuity that his system of three means of right knowledge does not, in fact, go against Gautama's system. Gautama first of five sense organ in the NS 1.1.12 and then in another place accepted the internal organs (mind) as the sixth sense organ. This shows that, according to Bhāsarvajña, Gautama's enumeration of items was not always meant to be exact or even mutually exclusive of other lists. Thus, although Gautama mentioned four means of right knowledge he would not have denied the fact that there are only three.[12] This argument is not satisfactory because it was criticised by the other Naiyāyikas who accept four means of right knowledge.[13]

The Prābhākara adds one more means of right knowledge, viz., persumption (*Arthāpatti*) to the list of means of right knowledge. Their argument is that when we learn something and find it difficult to understand because of incompatibility we assume something else in order to understand it. It is different from inference, while in inference the probans (*Hetu*) cannot exist in the subject unless the probandum (*Sādhya*) does, in presumption the relation is reserved; the probandum cannot exist in the subject unless the probans does.

The Bhāṭṭa adds on more, viz., non-apprehension, to the list of means of right knowledge. The knowledge about non-existence of an object is got through the non-apprehension. Paurāṇikas accept concurrence (*Saṁbhava*) and Tradition (*Aitihya*) also as distinct means of right knowledge. But the Mīmāṁsaka rejects special status to them as distinct means of knowledge on the following grounds; concurrence is knowledge of a part derived from knowledge of the whole but this is merely a kind of inference. (e.g. since there are a thousand people in the room, there are a hundred people also). Tradition is verbal testimony if it is true, and not a means at all if it is not. Therefore six only are the means of right knowledge. Here the *Rāmāyaṇa* also supports the six fold theory of means of knowledge, thus, 'O Rāma! in the world there are six means of knowledge by which, everything is comprehended.[14]

II. Prābhākara View

It is said that a thing or principle can be established by definitions and means of right knowledge and not by a mere statement (*na hi pratijñāmātreṇa vastusiddhiḥ. lakṣaṇapramāṇābhyāṁ vastusiddhiḥ*),[15] or that the establishment of an object of knowledge depends upon the means of right knowledge (*mānādhīnā meyasiddhiḥ*). Śālikanātha says that there are conflicting views among the philosophers as regards the number of means of right knowledge, etc., though the establishment of the object of knowledge is the common feature of all the Indian philosophy.[16]

As described above, the word., *'Pramāṇa'* has two meanings : (1) *Pramā* or right knowledge and (2) *Pramā-Karaṇa* or means of right knowledge. The Bhāṭṭas follow the latter meaning, i.e., means of right knowledge and the Prābhākaras follow the former, i.e., right knowledge. Śālikanātha defines *Pramāṇa* as follows, 'experience is right knowledge and it is something different from memory' (*anubhūtiḥ pramāṇaṁ sā smṛteranyā*).[17] Memory is regarded as invalid knowledge in as much as it stands in need of a previous knowledge. According to the Prābhākara, it is not necessary condition of validity of knowledge that its object should be one that is not already known.

One may ask there that his definition is too comprehensive (*Ativyāpta*) as it includes error under knowledge. The reply of the Prābhākara to this is that there is not error at all, but what passes for error as two knowledges, occurring consequently neither of which is itself erroneous. Of the knowledges, one is perceptual and other is recollective as in that of a piece of necre mistaken for silver (*śūkti- rajata*). We only forget that they are two knowledges. Actually speaking there is not wrong knowledge at all.[18]

The controversy centres around the question whether a right knowledge is necessarily a new piece of information. The Prābhākara is emphatic in answering the question in the negative and the Bhāṭṭa in answering in the affirmative. The Prābhākara contends that if a means of right knowledge is rightly employed in knowing a thing, the following knowledge must be deemed valid, irrespective of whether the features thus known in the thing are familiar to us or not; the Bhāṭṭa answers back by arguing that a thing as associated with one moment must work differently from the same thing as associated with another moment, not to take knowledge of an unfamiliar feature in a thing means not to acquire right knowledge concerning this thing.

III. Conclusion

As it has become obvious to us by now, the question is whether memory is a case of right knowledge or not. The Prābhākara divides all knowledges into those of the nature of memory and those not of the nature of memory but, unlike the Bhāṭṭa, he refuses to further subdivide the non-mnetic into right, wrong, doubt, etc., and maintained that the non-mnetic knowledge is the nature of right knowledge. The number of means of right knowledge recognized by the systems of Indian Philosophy as follows[19] (1) The Materialists accept only one, viz., perception (2) the Vaiśeṣikas and the Buddhists accept two viz., perception, and inference (3) The Sāṁkhyas accept three, viz., perception, inference and verbal testimony. (4) The Naiyāyikas recognize four, viz., perception, inference, verbal testimony and analogy (5) The Bhāṭṭas sanction six., viz., perception, inference, verbal testimony, analogy, presumption and non-apprehension. The Paurāṇikas add two more to the list, viz., probability (*Saṁbhava,)* and *Tradition (Aitihya*). The Prābhākaras, however, establish only five means of right knowledge, since they show that tradition can be included in verbal testimony, and probability in inference, and non-aprehension is superfluous.

REFERENCES

1. औत्पत्तिकस्तु शब्दस्यार्थेन । JS I-1-5.
2. PV 1-1; अविसंवादकं ज्ञानं सम्यग्ज्ञानम् । NBT p. 17.
3. KK. p. 102.
4. प्रमाकरणं प्रमाणम् अत्र च प्रमाणं लक्ष्यं,प्रमाकरणं लक्षणम् । TB. p. 1
5. तस्माद् दृशं यदुत्पन्नं नापि संवादमृक्षति ।
   ज्ञानान्तरेण विज्ञानं तत्प्रमाणं प्रतीयताम् ॥ SV. p. 103
6. SP. p. 45.
7. SP p. 45.
8. चार्वाकास्तावदेकं द्वितयमपि पुन... MM. p. 19.
9. प्रत्यक्षमनुमानञ्च प्रमाणं हि द्विलक्षणम् । Pramāṇasamuccaya, Ist Chapter.
10. वाक्यानि स्व स्मारितार्थसंसर्गवान्ति,आकांक्षाद्युत्पादकशक्तिमत्वात् ।
11. Nyāya Saṁgraha vārttika p. 6.
12. Nyāya Samgraha vārttika, Nyāyasūtra, p. 81.
13. NS. 1-1-4.
14. The Ramāyaṇa of Vālmīki, Araṇya Kāṇḍa. 52-8.
15. Quoted for example JNMV 1-1-2.
16. PP. p. 122.
17. PP. p. 127.
18. ननु शुक्तिकायां रजतमिदमिति ज्ञानं । PP. p. 152.
19. NSM. PP, p. 112.